This page intentionally left blank

New Brighton – A Victorian Seaside Resort

By Tony Franks-Buckley

Dedication

This book is dedicated to all my friends and family who have supported me through my life and help me achieve the goals that I have reached. I also dedicate it to my loved ones who are gone but not forgotten.

Joyce Dennett

Norman Spearing

Derek Franks

Mabel Buckley

Acknowledgements

I would like to thank my family who have supported me through tough times and good times especially my Mum and my best friend Uncle John. I would also like to thank those that have educated me and allowed me to become the person that I am today. And last but not least I would like to thank Gavin Chappell. Whose previous work on Pirates in the area has helped me considerably.

About the Author

Wallasey Historian and Author that completed a BA Honors Degree in Modern History at Liverpool John Moores University under the guidance of fellow author Prof Frank McDonough, Dr Mike Benbough-Jackson and a host of others.

Main interests in history are from the Industrial Revolution era in Britain, which was the beginning of the modern day Britain as we know it today. Also holds a keen interest in World War II due to learning from Uncle, who served in the Royal Navy and was involved in the D-Day landings.

As well as graduating from university, previously attended Wirral Metropolitan College in Birkenhead and gained A Level results through an Access to Higher Education Diploma in English Literature, History and Environmental Studies which allowed advancement to University.

Other Books and Research Papers

The History of Wallasey – A Small Suburb with a Large History

The History of Birkenhead & Bidston

Liverpool during the Industrial Revolution 1700 – 1850

To What Extent did the EU Unite Europe by the end of the 20th Century?

Was the Great British Reform Act of 1832 Truly "Great"?

How effective were poor law reforms and philanthropy in reducing the causes of poverty in Britain during the 19th Century?

Was there an "American Indian Holocaust" from English Migration to America?

How effective was Nazi Propaganda?

To what extent did Britain experience an "Agricultural Revolution" between 1750 – 1830?

Globalization in the Modern World.

Find me on Twitter @TonyFrBuckley

My Blog Site http://tonyfranksbuckley.blogspot.co.uk/

What was special about the British Seaside?

Miles of Animation at New Brighton

Most of our ideas of the British, and especially the English and Welsh, seaside resorts are all the stronger for having our own Victorian roots. For it was the working class movements during the time of Queen Victoria's reign, that created the need to have an area for leisurely entertainment. The Seaside became a popular destination for many, not only the upper class, but the middle and lower as well.

The larger Victorian resorts, such as New Brighton, Blackpool, and Brighton. Catered for the rapidly-expanding working-class holiday market of the late nineteenth century, most obviously New

Brighton and Blackpool offered 'pleasure palaces. They combined music-hall, variety and dancing with a broader menu which might include zoos, opera houses, theatres, aquariums, lagoons with Venetian gondolas and gondoliers, pleasure gardens and1 exhibitions. This kind of provision reached its apotheosis in Blackpool's Tower and Winter Gardens, and in the even more ambitious Tower at New Brighton, a financial failure which was demolished soon after the First World War. (See Picture below)

Such large-scale commercial entertainment's hardly paid satisfactory profits even in their heyday, outside of New Brighton

1 *Recreation and the Sea* edited by S Fisher (Exeter: University of Exeter Press, 1997)

and Blackpool2. They, along with the Victorian seaside hotels, such as Wellington road in New Brighton for instance, were particularly vulnerable to changes in popular taste and in the economics of the entertainment industry from the 1950s onwards. But they have their own contribution to make to the nostalgic appreciation of the Victorian seaside, in this case as somewhere popular, Somewhere where those who worked hard came to play even harder during their brief period of release, and spent their hard-earned sixpences on pioneering versions of what is known as 'mass entertainment'.

These different versions of seaside nostalgia remind us that there were and still are many versions of the British seaside.3 Little informal villages, where fishing and farming predominated and visitors entertained themselves and each other, up to big purpose-built holiday towns with the full inclusion of commercial entertainment and huge crowds of visitors, who needed policing as well as pleasing. Whose presence had to be supported by comprehensive and expensive local government systems providing whatever private enterprise could not, would not or (Victorians thought) should not provide at a profit, from drains and gasworks to tramways, promenades and even orchestras.

The celebrations of seaside innocence have to reckon with not only the weather and the ever-present scope for discord within families, but also with the problems that arose when visitors with clashing values and expectations about what constituted legitimate holiday fun came into close and sometimes abrasive holiday proximity. The seaside as relaxing, informal escape from the pressures of the daily grind might also be compromised by the demands of the

2 *The Blackpool landlady: A Social History* by JK Walton (Manchester University Press, 1978)
3 *The English Seaside Resort: A Social History 1750-1914* by J K Walton, (Leicester University Press, 1983)

promenade, of fashion, personal display, flirtation and consumption, at least in the larger resorts.

Victorian holidaymakers4 were thoroughly 'modern' in their recognition and sometimes, the enjoyment of such imperatives. They did not have to reckon with the problems of bodily exposure and the conflicts between fashion and morality that sunbathing was to bring in the new century, as they sheltered beneath their parasols to protect their milky complexions.

But bathing and its regulation, through the attempted imposition and widespread evasion of the regime of separating the sexes and charging for the use of the horse-drawn wooden 'bathing-machine' with its protective 'modesty-hood', provided quite enough controversy in its absence.

---

4 *The Englishman's Holiday: A Social History* by JAR Pimlott (Flare Books, 1976, first published 1947)

To add extra spice to this mixture, the Victorian years saw the first widespread large-scale expansion of English and Welsh seaside resorts, and growing pains often exacerbated social and cultural conflict, especially as the market for holidays broadened to include significant numbers first of clerks and shopkeepers, then the industrial working class.

The seaside resort was an eighteenth-century inventiputs as 'orthodox' medicine put a 'scientific' vencostumespopular sea-bathing customs and marketed the result as a supplement or (increasingly) alternative to 'taking the cure' at a spa, while new romantic ways of perceiving shoreline made them attractive where hitherto they had repelled, running parallel with the revolution in taste that drew the fashionable and cultivated to the Lake District and the Alps.

Brighton 5 could already count 40,000 inhabitants, most of them permanently, at the June census of 1841. But growth on the grand scale began with the railway age, as the railways boosted existing small settlements (they very rarely started new resorts from scratch) by making access cheaper in time and money. The main beneficiaries around mid-century were middle-class families, from the substantial to the struggling, despite the relative anonymity of resort settings, especially in southern England, allowed young bachelors in mundane employment to reinvent themselves and go on the spree for a fortnight.

Over most of the country, working-class visitors relied on cheap excursions, organised by Sunday Schools, employers, temperance societies or commercial promoters, among whom Thomas Cook was as unimportant as were the penny-a-mile Parliamentary trains

---

5 *Brighton: Old Ocean's Bauble* by EW Gilbert (Flare Books, 1975, first published 1954)

under the Act of 1844,6 which charged more and took longer than the 'cheap trips'. Here are myths that need dispelling. Only from the 1870s onwards did the Lancashire cotton workers take the lead in developing a genuine working-class seaside holiday system, saving through the year to convert the traditional Wakes holidays (unpaid for most until after the Second World War) into seaside breaks, and changing the character of many northern resorts in the process. Londoners, like, for example, Sheffield folk and coal miners, depended more on 'St Monday', that enduring but an unofficial extension of the weekend. They also used August Bank Holiday, 'St Lubbock's Day' after its inventor in 1871, as it became a popular holiday from the mid-1870s; but the importance of this has also been greatly inflated, and it was irrelevant in most of the north and midlands.

But by the last quarter of the nineteenth century many of the more accessible resorts were having to cope with the novelty of a working-class presence of growing dimensions and spending power, especially young people with wages and few responsibilities, and older men who lacked family commitments or chose to cast them aside. Here was a recipe for potential strife, and the popular media of the time, from Punch to Ally Sloper's Half Holiday, added jokes about cultural conflict between the classes to their older staples about clerks and shop assistants pretending to be gentlemen, adding a new dimension to the comedy of social embarrassment.7

The sheer variety of resort environments, which itself contributed to the ubiquitous popularity of the seaside by offering all things to all the people, it was also clearly understood by the humorists.

---

6 *Power and Politics at the Seaside* by N Morgan and A Pritchard (University of Exeter Press, 2000)
7 *The English Seaside Resort: A Social History 1750-1914* by J K Walton, (Leicester University Press, 1983)

They depicted Brighton as a carnival of strange juxtapositions between fashionable high society and its imitators and an exotic medley of Cockney trippers and vulgar, assertive stallholders and alfresco entertainers.

The mainstream family resorts with their importunate minstrels and sly fishermen offered gentle comedies combining displacement, routine, discomfort and boredom, while the little fishing villages that catered for the alternative fashion for the picturesque, untidy and informal were theatres of misunderstanding between the patronising and the patronised, with the latter usually having fun at the expense of the former. The spice was added by the visitors' painful awareness that nothing was as innocent as it might seem, as landladies and boatmen strove to extract the last penny from their summer bonanza by bending and stretching their rules of engagement.

All these perceptions reflected the 'luminal' nature of the seaside as a gateway between land and sea, culture and nature, civilized constraint and liberated hedonism. The spirit of carnival bubbled close to the surface, threatening and promising to turn the world 'upside down' as the holiday atmosphere stimulated the latent fun, laughter and suspension of inhibitions that Dickens celebrated in his readers.[8]

These influences fought against the internal drives towards staid respectability, and fear of embarrassment that were also so strong in Victorian culture, especially among the lower middle classes. Local authorities, drawing the line in different places according to their perceptions of their markets, had to pay heed to drive for the control and suppression of levity that tended to carry greater political clout. Respectability was as contentious a fault-line as the

[8] *Leisure in Britain 1780-1939* edited by JK Walton and J Walvin (Manchester University Press, 1983)

class in the conflicts that cut across the enjoyment and tranquillity of the Victorian seaside. It was all the more sharply contested because its definitions were uncertain at the core as well as the edges. Alongside bathing regulation, Sunday observance was a particular touchstone. In these respects as in many others, escape to the seaside brought with it the conflicts and uneasiness about morality and identity which were so pervasive in Victorian life for the rest of the year.

Contents

INTRODUCTION

New Brighton is a British seaside resort forming part of the town of Wallasey, in the Metropolitan Borough of Wirral, in the metropolitan county of Merseyside, England. It is located at the north-eastern tip of the Wirral Peninsula, within the historic county boundaries of Cheshire, and has sandy beaches which line the Irish Sea. At the 2001 Census, the population of the electoral ward of New Brighton stood at 14,450 (6,869 males, 7,581 females)9

---

9 *2001 Census: New Brighton*, Office for National Statistics, retrieved 19 November 2012

Up to the 19th century, the area had a reputation for smuggling and wrecking, and secret underground cellars and tunnels are still rumoured to exist. It also had a strategic position at the entrance to the Mersey Estuary.

The Perch Rock battery was completed in 1829. It mounted 18 guns, mostly 32 pounders, with 3 6-inch guns installed in 1899. Originally cut off at high tide, coastal reclamation has since made it fully accessible.

In 1830, a Liverpool merchant, James Atherton, purchased much of the land at Rock Point, which enjoyed views out to sea and across the Mersey and had a good beach. His aim was to develop it as a desirable residential and watering place for the gentry, in a similar way to Brighton, one of the most elegant seaside resorts of that Regency period – hence "New Brighton". Substantial development began soon afterwards, and housing began to spread up the hillside overlooking the estuary – a former gunpowder magazine being closed down in 1851.

During the latter half of the 19th century, New Brighton developed as a very popular seaside resort serving Liverpool and the Lancashire industrial towns, and many of the large houses were converted to inexpensive hotels. A pier was opened in the 1860s, and the promenade from Seacombe to New Brighton was built in the 1890s. This served both as a recreational amenity in its own right, and to link up the developments along the estuary, and was later extended westwards towards Leasowe. The New Brighton Tower, the tallest in the country, was opened in 1900 but closed in 1919, largely due to lack of maintenance during World War I. Dismantling of the tower was complete by 1921.

After World War II, the popularity of New Brighton as a seaside resort declined dramatically. However, the Tower Ballroom continued as a major venue, hosting numerous concerts in the 1950s and 1960s by local Liverpool groups such as The Beatles as well as other international stars. The Tower Ballroom continued in use until it was destroyed by a fire in 1969.

Ferries across the Mersey to New Brighton ceased in 1971, after which the ferry pier and landing stage were dismantled. By 1977, the promenade pier had suffered the same fate. The area became the subject of Martin Parr's famous and controversial photographic book *The Last Resort*. The town was also the birthplace of writer Malcolm Lowry.

New Brighton is part of the Wallasey parliamentary constituency and represented by Angela Eagle MP, of the Labour Party who retained her seat in the 2010 general election.

New Brighton is an electoral ward of the Metropolitan Borough of Wirral, which is itself a district of the metropolitan county of Merseyside. Elections for Wirral Council took place on 6 May 2010: Patricia Glasman (Labour) 3,072 votes. Bill Duffey (Conservative) 2,173. Julia Codling (LD) 1,166. Cynthia Stonall (Green Party) 342. Timothy Pass (UKIP) 222. (Electorate: 11,025 Turnout: 63.6 percent – Majority: 899)

New Brighton has a wide range of visitor attractions and facilities. These focus on the £60m Marine Point Leisure and Retail development completed in 2011. This includes The Light 8 Screen digital multiplex cinema, a Travelodge hotel, a range of cafe bars and restaurants, a G Casino, a Morrison's supermarket and a sailing school using the refurbished Marine Lake. Other attractions include the Riverside Bowl bowling alley, the Laser Quest centre, the Art-Deco New Palace Amusement Arcade (which includes a small fairground) and the Floral Pavilion Theatre which was rebuilt in 2008 as a first phase of the Town's regeneration and accommodates a Conference Centre. Significant investment has also been made in the public realm with particular highlights being a model boating lake and the Promenade.

The four-mile-long (six kilometres) North Wirral Coastal Park is situated between New Brighton and Meols. The Wirral Show, a free-to-enter annual event, was held on the open ground of the King's Parade in New Brighton. In 2009 it was announced that after 33 years, The Wirral Show was to be axed. There is a minor club scene in the town, with *RJ's* and the *Playas' Lounge* (both now closed) replaced by I-Kandi and soon to be a Lloyds Bar on the seafront, and *the Tavern* further inland.

The pop concert *New Brighton Rock* was held over two days: 21 and 22 May 1984 at the town's open-air swimming pool and transmitted by Granada Television on 23 June 1984 on ITV. It featured many musical artists of the day including Frankie Goes to Hollywood, Gloria Gaynor, Madness, Nik Kershaw and Spandau Ballet. A strain was placed on local police resources due to an on-going commitment to the 1984–85 miners' strike. Nevertheless, the event was covered by Merseyside Police's Wirral Division.

A song about New Brighton called "New Brighton" was included on the 1992 album *Song* by Liverpool-based group it's Immaterial. In 1996, Wallasey Brit-pop band The Boo Radleys released the *C'mon Kids* album. Track 9 on the album was an atmospheric and nostalgic song called "New Brighton Promenade". New Brighton is briefly mentioned in the song "Radio America" by The Libertines and there is also a song "New Brighton" by Pete Doherty.

The Bandstand situated in Vale Park is a popular outdoor music venue, hosting a variety of acts, typically an orchestra or choir every Sunday. In more recent times, the bandstand has hosted music to a much younger generation and popular throughout the summer. It has been an ideal platform for local bands wanting to gain recognition.

Vale Park, showing New Band Stand, New Brighton

New Brighton Tower F.C. was an association football League club based in New Brighton that folded in 1901. Like Liverpool, Chelsea and Thames, New Brighton Tower was formed to play at an already-built stadium, the Tower Athletic Grounds, with a massive capacity of 80,000. The owners of the New Brighton Tower, a seaside attraction built to rival the Blackpool Tower, decided there was a need to provide winter entertainment, and had built a stadium adjacent to the tower. The football club was formed in 1896 to provide the entertainment, and joined the Lancashire League at the start of the 1897-98 seasons. After finishing as champions in their first season, the club was elected to the Second Division of the Football League when the League was expanded by four clubs. The team was very poorly supported, often averaging gates of 1,000.

The club signed a number of new players, including some who had played international football, and was reasonably successful, finishing 5th (out of 18) in its first season, and 4th in their third season. However, the cost of maintaining a professional football club became too high for the Tower's owners, and the club was disbanded in the summer of 1901, and replaced in the League by Doncaster Rovers.

In 1921, a new club was formed, New Brighton A.F.C., who would also play in the Football League from 1923 until 1951.

New Brighton is one of the smallest settlements ever to have a Football League club, although it was in close proximity to the much larger Liverpool.

The Early Years

WRECKERS & SMUGGLERS

The wrecking of shipping was widespread on the Wirral Coast, especially in Wallasey. Stonehouse wrote in 1863 about the wreckers and the smuggling that went on by those who were farm labourers by day and wreckers by night. In fact, a local saying was:-

"Wallasey for wreckers
Poulton for trees
Liscard for honest men
And Seacombe for thieves".

The last Wallasey wreck occurred in 1904. Reports say that in the early hours of 30th December wreckers lit fires to decoy the 'Ulloa' on to the sandbanks, The 'Ulloa', from Barcelona, was loaded with fruit and wines. She failed to pick up a pilot and swept on to the hidden Burbo Bank. The crew were taken off, but for three weeks until a great gale blew up, the master, Captain Oleaga, stayed on his 600-ton ship.

Dawn visitors to the shore found cases of oranges and lemons and literally within minutes, four-fifths of the population - to quote one eyewitness - were marching towards the shore. The news spread to Birkenhead and Liverpool and the fruits washed up by the sea were quickly placed into containers of every conceivable size and shape. Many brought handcarts and wheelbarrows. It became known as 'Orange Week' on account of the amount of oranges. Meanwhile, police, coastguard's and Customs officers arrived and calm reigned - until barrels of the finest vintage wines were spotted. They were plotted and seized by the officers the moment they hit the shore, but there were many casualties as people stabbed penknives and gimlets into the barrels. Gushing fountains of wine were transferred into all sorts of containers - including empty orange skins. The gale still blew bringing in more and more containers including casks of rum and sherry.

PIRATES AND SMUGGLERS IN NEW BRIGHTON

Before New Brighton was called "New Brighton" it was nothing more than beaches and rocks. It held several names such as "Perch Rock" or even "Ye Black Rock" But what has hardly ever been covered by historians throughout modern history, is its association with pirates & smugglers, who frequented the area for personal gain, taking advantage of the busy shipping lane of the River Mersey.

Although mostly associated with Cornwall, smuggling was a common occupation in poor seaside communities along all the coasts of Britain. Like many forms of crimes, it came about as the result of legislature, when Edward 1 placed a customs duty of wool exports to Europe, a duty that increased throughout the Hundred Years War, in order to fund the king's attempts to become King of France. He customs service was primarily concerned with collecting duties, but as time went on, illegal trade increased, particularly in the 17th and 18th centuries when smuggling reached industrial proportions. Wool exports were criminalised in 1614, and made punishable by death in 1661.[10] Smugglers began to arm themselves against the dreaded Revenue men, who were soon provided with 'cutters' to patrol the coasts. (Wirral Smugglers, Wreckers & Pirates - Gavin Chappell)

Wallasey forms the northerly corner of the Wirral and has always been somewhat remote from the remainder of the Wirral. A town without a centre, visitors had difficulty finding their way about; locals prided themselves in being a breed apart. In the 18th and 19th Centuries all of North Wirral was remote and cut off from more densely populated areas.

Wallasey was more isolated than most and it gained a notorious reputation as a haunt of smugglers and pirates. The headquarters of

---

10 Wirral Smugglers, Wreckers & Pirates - Gavin Chappell

local smuggling was a house that once stood on the river front between Lincoln Drive and Caithness Drive on what is now Egremont Promenade. Built in 1595 by one of the Mainwaring family beside what was at that time Liscard Moor, on the high water mark of the River Mersey, it went through a number of different names including the Half Way House, The Whitehouse and Seabank Nook. Next to it were 3 houses, some of which remain, called Seabank Cottages. The house became a tavern during the American War of Independence, when American and English privateers roamed the ocean and John Paul Jones raided Whitehaven in Cumbria.

The tavern gained the nick name Mother Redcap's after Poll Jones, who always wore a red cap or bonnet. Its normal title was The Half Way House. It was officially this until late into the 19th century.

One of the ports of call of the Smugglers transferring contraband across Bidston Moss was the Ring 'o Bells, now Stone Farm, in Bidston. Owned by a local family, some say the Radley's, others the Pendleton's. In the mid 19th Century Mary Radley or Pendleton married a Simon Croft under which the Ring 'o Bells became as notorious as Mother Redcap's. It also had a well established reputation for Ham 'n Eggs! It is described in The Adventures of Christopher Tadpole! Simon Croft kept his own pigs but became something of a drunkard. A lively and mixed crowd used the establishment including prize fighters Tom Sayers, Jem Mace and 'Tipton Slasher'. Four years after his death, in 1864, Lady Cust (Leasowe Castle) prevailed upon Squire Vyner, the lord of the manor, to revoke the licence. Bidston has been 'dry' ever since. Sept 2010. Note: I have had an email from Victoria Hart who tells me that the pub was indeed a Radley pub. She goes on: I can confirm that it was Mary Radley who married Simon Croft. Mary and Simon are buried together in St Oswald's cemetery. . I also know that the Inn was originally nicknamed the Ham and Bacon house as the Radley's would cure their own ham and they were carefully preserved from damp.

On occasion revenue men may be found to be waiting near the moss for contraband. In such cases, the contraband was taken along the edge of the Moss and around to Saughall Massie, to a Mill, which stood in what is now Action Lane, Moreton. One such tale relates that a revenue man lay in wait as he had been tipped off that two barrels of rum were to be carried that night across the Moss to the Ring 'o Bells. As the carter approached the Revenue man leapt out of hiding and challenged the carter. You have rum in those kegs!! Nay, its ale - the Ring o' Bells has run out and I'm taking them some. On checking contents, it was indeed ale. The smugglers had got wind of the revenue man and switched the rum barrels for ale!!

Another instance was when Revenue men saw two men removing bales from the area of a wreck. After a pursuit, the bales were found to contain cabbages and ferns. The real stolen bales had vanished by the time the Revenue men returned to the shore. Mother Redcaps finally closed its doors in 1960 after an unsuccessful short lived nightclub venture, and was demolished in October 1974. During demolition the famous 'smuggler's well' was discovered by the workmen, they found lots of bottles, jars and flagons and they wanted to inform the museum authorities! The foreman insisted that the 'hole' be filled in and treasures of lost artefacts were found were lost again. He threatened to sack anybody who told the museum! Sadly there are too many of these short sighted idiots around and much has been destroyed here and elsewhere that could have been saved. Maybe the foreman had found something he would rather not be made public? Who knows? (*Information taken from Wirral Smugglers, Wreckers & Pirates, a 2009 publication by Gavin Chappell which is on sale at local bookshops and Amazon.*)

The prayer of the Wirral Wreckers was tragically answered on many occasions. At the foot of the old Wallasey Parish Church tower lie two weather worn and almost forgotten gravestones, concealing a tale of one such shipwreck on the Wirral shore. An apt resting place, looking out, as it does, over Leasowe Castle and the Wirral shore, the waters of Liverpool Bay and the very sandbank where disaster struck. On Christmas Day, 1838, the packet ship "Pennsylvania" set sail from Liverpool bound for New York. She proceeded to the mouth of the Mersey to await the first favourable wind. She was a superior and fast sailing freight carrying vessel, with cabins commodious and elegantly fitted.

On this voyage there were 40 people on board, of which 5 were passengers. On the 12th day of Christmas, a Sunday, she finally put to sea on her fatal voyage. It was 10.30am and there was already a strong wind blowing from the southeast. The ship had a good run as far as Point Lynas, off Anglesey, which she reached by 9pm. Then she was totally becalmed for some 10 minutes, the proverbial lull before the storm.

The wind freshened from the southeast, and soon after midnight the Pennsylvania was in the midst of a hurricane. It was the 13th day of Christmas. The storm continued unabated throughout the Monday. About the Pennsylvania efforts were made to clear the damage, and turn the ship about. When daylight came on Tuesday, Captain Smith, her Commander, tried to put back to Liverpool. On reaching Ormes Head, a course was plotted for the Mersey Lightship. Unknown to the Pennsylvania, however, the floating light had parted from its mooring the previous day. Normally it was anchored off the East Hoyle Bank to help guide mariners safely into the Horse and Rock Channels.

The newspapers of the time were suspicious:

"To say the violence of the gale drove her from her moorings is absurd. The floating light .... makes its appearance .... so regularly in the Mersey with every onslaught of the elements...... (That one might suspect) those who tended it felt so deeply for their own personal safety in times of danger that they quit their post. Again, during the past gale when most needed to guide vessels in distress, has this vessel parted her moorings. It is scarcely two months since she parted her moorings before a gale and came into port. To us this is very extraordinary and inexplicable"

The Pennsylvania still bewildered by the absence of the Lightship, dropped anchor off Hoylake, about three miles from the shore. It was now 1.30pm on Tuesday. Before another anchor could be dropped however, the vessel swung around, drifted, and struck the Hoyle Bank. The force of the gale rammed her into the bank 8 or 9 times, and she started to take on water rapidly. Strangely, two other packet ships, the St Andrew and the Lockwoods also struck the Bank, not more than half a mile apart. One cannot help but recall the words of James Stonehouse, writing in 1863:

"Many a fierce fire has been lighted on the Wirral shore on stormy nights to lure the good ship onto the Burbo or Hoyle Banks, there to beat and strain and throb, until her timbers parted ...."

In an attempt to reach the shore, the Pennsylvania's jolly boat was launched into the gale. Aboard it were 5 passengers, including one William Douglas, as well as the Chief Mate, Lucas B Blydenburgh, and several of the crew. Those worn gravestones in a Wallasey churchyard tell only too well the fate of that little boat. Only one of its occupants survived. Meanwhile back on the wreck of the Pennsylvania, the long boat, the only other prospect of escape, was lost in heavy waves, which also swept the Captain overboard. It was 3pm Tuesday.

Much of the hull was now underwater. The remaining crew climbed desperately into the rigging where they were to cling for dear life for 19 hours. It was not until 10 am the next day that the steam tug Victoria took them off, except that is, three of the crew who had literally been starved to death of cold and hunger in the rigging during the night. 21 were saved from the wreck, 19 drowned. From the wreckers of the Wirral shore, the storm had come as a belated Christmas present. Liverpool newspapers commented:

"We lament finding that these infamous wretches, the wreckers, have been at their fiendlike occupation, plundering what the elements have spared, instead of seeking to alleviate the calamities of their fellow creatures. The wreckers who infest the Cheshire coast were not long in rendering the catastrophe a source of emolument to themselves. The property of the passengers and crew where plundered by them to an alarming extent. The Steward, who had in his trunk, sixty watches and other articles of jewellery, found on regaining the vessel that the whole of it had disappeared". Some reports placed the value of the cargoes carried by the Pennsylvania and St Andrew as high as £400,000, so it is hardly surprising that the wreckers chose the Pennsylvania as their "especial prey". The Pennsylvania had suffered, most her state cabin has almost entirely been stripped.

A number of plunderers were, however, taken into custody. One in particular, a John Bibby, boatman, is worthy of our interest. When apprehended he was found to have forty yards of new cloth, valued at £12, folded round his body. In his fishing boat were found books, a large and handsome cruet stand, and a black coat, a pair of trousers, a pair of drawers and much else.

It transpired that the coat had belonged to the late Captain Smith and the cruet stand to the same ship. The trousers belonged to Mr Thompson, its sole surviving passenger. The owner of the drawers was never ascertained. Bibby claimed in court that the cloth had been given him by a man on the Pier Head. Nor had he any idea how the other articles had found their way into his boat. He was fined £27. In default of payment he was to be jailed for 6 months. He might have considered himself lucky, for it was an age when a not unknown penalty for wrecking was public whipping or even transportation. William Douglas, one of the 5 passengers, who along with the First and Second Mates, tried to escape from the wreck. However, the ill fated boat did not live long in the tempest. About midway between the vessel and shore, she swamped, and all on board was thrown into the sea. He succeeded in reaching the shore, he was immediately taken to Leasowe Castle but he only survived a short time. The Captain and First and Second Mates were also drowned. It was thus reported,

"His mortal remains (Lucas Blydenburgh) were attended to the grave by all American Captains in port, as well as by hundreds of seamen. The sight was most mournful "The Inscription reads:"Sacred to the memory of Lucas B Blydenburgh of New York, Mate of the Packet Ship Pennsylvania, who was drowned near Leasowe Castle after leaving the wreck during the Memorable Gale on January the 8th 1839. Aged 40 years"

Max Moeller Director of Research Services The Historical Society of Pennsylvania 1300 Locust St. Philadelphia, PA 19107 has replied to a question from me asking about ships images, he states that: I have found two images reproduced in published sources (both of which should still be available in bookstores) of the U.S. Ship Pennsylvania . Neither of the originals is owned by HSP.

They are:11 "Launch of the U.S. Ship Pennsylvania", a wood engraving by R.S. Gilbert, July 1837 – private collection (reproduction found on page 271 of Russell Weigley's *Philadelphia: A 300 Year History, 1982*); and "View of the Launch of the U.S. Ship of War Pennsylvania", lithograph by Lehman & Duval after G. Lehman, 1837 – Library of Congress (reproduction in Edwin Wolfe's *Philadelphia: Portrait of an American City, 1990*).

The following extract is taken from the book "Portrait of Wirral" by "Kenneth Burnley".

One hundred and fifty years ago this stretch of coast was renowned for its wreckers; robbers and smugglers who would lure the Liverpool-bound vessels on to the sandbanks using decoy lights and flares. Once ashore, the wreckers showed no mercy towards the unfortunate crew and passengers; if their lives were spared, their cargoes and belongings were not. But not all wrecking was deliberate; winter storms claimed many ships, and local people

---

11 Philadelphia: A 300 Year History, 1982, Russell Weigley

were quick to arrive on the scene to salvage what they could. Henry Aspinall, of Birkenhead, wrote this vivid description of a severe storm in 1839: On 6th January 1839, the day was fine; a fair wind blew for outward-bound ships. Many left the Mersey under sail, among them the St Andrew, the Lockwoods, and the Pennsylvania, first class packet ships, loaded with valuable cargoes and emigrants together with a few saloon passengers for New York. On the morning of the 7th, the barometer fell to a very low point. The vessels had almost reached Holyhead, when suddenly the wind changed to the north-west and blew a hurricane. The three vessels at once put back for the Mersey, the only shelter in such a gale. Unfortunately the wind veered dead north-west, and took the three vessels on to the Burbo and West Hoyle Banks. The sea rose to a fearful height, and the vessels settled in the sand until they were literally smashed to pieces. No boats could live. The moment they reached the water they were swamped and all on board were washed away. Many were drowned and washed ashore at Leasowe, Hoylake, and the neighbouring coast. Such a sight I never saw before or since, nor should I like to. The scene deeply impressed. The beach was covered with wreckage and dead bodies. I vividly recall the latter. It was, indeed, a most pitiful sight. To this day, in old Hoylake cottages, may be seen cupboards, doors, satinwood fittings, and glass and ebony door handles, washed up and appropriated by the finders, sad relics of a catastrophe which caused a great sensation in the district.

MOTHER REDCAPS

Mother Redcaps is undoubtedly one of Wallasey's most famous land marks. The old white-washed, short; stumpy looking building was built by the Mainwaring family in 1595 on the river bank. It was a bold stone building with walls nearly three feet thick. The house was known by many names over the century's, names such as the Halfway House, the White House, Seabank Nook and several others.

The name Mother Redcaps came about in the 1700's when an elderly lady in her autumn years was the owner and proprietor of the tavern, and was well known for always wearing a red hood or cap. The tavern was frequented by sea farer's and smugglers as it was well known that Mother Redcap was trustworthy and allowed contraband to be hidden within the tavern, albeit I am sure for a fee or cut of the profit. The activities of mother red cap over the years are well documented and in essence, she provided the first bank service to appear in Wallasey. She would store goods and currency within the building and sometimes even pay out prize money to the locals of which was be trusted to her as a neutral party.

The actual building looked like no more than a small white cottage, although this was the image that she wanted to portray; however inside it was a far different matter. Accounts shows that the front door was made of solid oak, five inches thick, studded with square headed nails. The remains of the door, although much decayed, were found in the cellar by Mr Kitchingman when making alterations in 1888. There were indications of it having had several sliding bars across the inside, and slots were also found at the sides of the lower windows as though at one time strong shutters had been fitted to them.

Immediately on the inside of the door was a trap door into the cellar under the north room. It would seem that by forcing the front door, it would withdraw the bolt to the trap door, thus letting the intruder fall eight or nine feet to the cellar floor, rendering them immobile at the very least. The way into this cellar was concealed by a rough wooden lid with the remains of hinges and shackles at the sides and entry could be gained from the back of the staircase in the passage from the south to the north room. Under the house stairs seven or eight steps led down into this cellar. If the front door lid or trap were down, the visitor, unless he turned to the right or left into the south or north front room, would proceed (there being no lobby) straight upstairs, and if anyone were in the cellar at the time he could run up the steps under the staircase and get out at the back of the house, there being a narrow doorway at the top of the steps into the yard. When the front door was open the entrance to the south room was a closed by it.

Behind the stairs was a door leading to the old kitchen at the back of the house and so into the open backyard. In this yard was a well about twelve feet deep, dry and partly filled with earth. There

34

seemed to have been a hole made at the west side of the well, appearing to lead into the garden, but probably leading into a passage, to be referred to later. There was a small stream of good water at the back of the house, which supplied the house and also the small vessels that anchored off here. There was a primitive brew-house at the back, and even down to about 1840 the house was noted for its strong, home-brewed dark ale. There was another large cave or cellar at the south end of the house; indeed under the greenhouse (1930) it sounded hollow, and the coarse mosaic was laid on the top of large, flat, sandstone flags placed over this hollow. This cavity was entered by a square hole with steps as though it were an old dry pit well. Part of the yard was in reality the roof of a large cavern, composed of flagstones carried on beams.

On it stood a large manure heap, and a stock of coal and coal scales completed the disguise. This coal was supplied by flats and was retailed to the inhabitants of Liscard and Wallasey. When the cave was used for the reception of any goods that were better kept from the public gaze, the coals and a few odd barrels were manoeuvred so as to conceal the cavity, and the appearance of any disturbance of the ground was obliterated. At the end of this cave was a narrow underground passage (mentioned in some books as leading to the Red Noses) which led to a concealed opening in a ditch that ran down from the direction of Liscard. It is probable that this tunnel joined the one from the old well in the yard. The ditch was a deep cutting as far as a pit that was about halfway up what is now Lincoln Drive. At the edge of this pit grew a large willow tree, with long overhanging branches which formed an excellent concealed look-out commanding the entrance of the river. The trunk of this tree was sawn in sections in 1889, and when Lincoln Drive was cut through the pit, the root was rolled down the hill to the garden where for twenty-three years it formed a rude table in the summer-house. A cutting from this tree was planted by Mr Kitchingman in 1890 at the back of the house and grew higher than the house itself.

The beams inside the house on each side of the fireplace were of old oak, but as some were too decayed to keep they were removed; two, however, were retained. The one in the north room is quite sound, almost blue-black and as hard as steel. The chimney breasts are of great area inside, and in the two ground floor rooms were cavities (near the ceiling over the oak beams) with removable entrances from the top of the chimney breasts inside the flues.

In the south room there was a cavity hardly sufficient to conceal a person of more than small stature, the wall of which had to be pierced when Mr Kitchingman made the small staircase to the studio. There were a few other small cavities in the walls papered over where the sailors, it was said, hid their wages and share of prize-money. An artificial harbour stood next to the old cottage (1865) and remains still across, under the promenade. It formed a shelter for boats stored on its south side, and could be made higher by sliding boards between thick posts. Sometimes with a north-west gale and high tide the water flowed into the cellar.

There was a wooden seat across the strand in front of the house composed of thick timbers from wrecks. It had a short wooden flagstaff at one end with a large plain wooden vane at the top. This vane was supposed to work round with the wind but it was in reality a dummy; the staff fitting down into a round wooden socket in the shingle could be turned in any direction and was used by the smugglers for signalling. When the vane pointed to the house it meant 'Come on,' and when pointing away, 'Keep off.' At the other end of the seat was another post, with a sign hanging from it adorned with a portrait of Old Mother Redcap holding a frying pan on a painted fire, and underneath these words:

All ye that are weary come in an take rest,
Our eggs and our ham they are of the best,
Our ale and our porter are likewise the same,
Step in if you please and give 'em a name.
- Mother Redcap

This post acted as a kind of counterpoise to the vane. The old seat and sign were seen by Mr Kitchingman's father when, in his twentieth year (1820), he stayed there for a short time. When this house was built about 1596, rumour has it that it was the only building on the river front between the old Seacombe Ferry boathouse and the old herring curing house at Rock Point, now New Brighton. The house became a tavern in the Privateering days of 1778-90, and was much frequented by the officers and crews of the Privateers,2 the Redcap, 16 guns; Nemesis, 18 guns; Alligator, 16 guns; Racehorse, 14 guns; Ariet, 12 guns; and other small vessels made use of the good anchorage known as 'Red Bet's', opposite the house.

A single small cannon, punched with the broad arrow, was unearthed during Mr Kitchingman's alterations. It had a spike welded on the end to replace a wooden handle, long since decayed away, to turn the gun in the desired direction. It was evidently a bow-chaser from some Privateer. It was placed by Mr Kitchingman in his garden, together with the remains of two flint muskets found near, and of about the same date.

Another interesting find was a 'Nine-hole stone', supported by a pedestal of brick. Nine Holes is a French game, halfpence being thrown at the holes, and was the forerunner of bagatelle. It was supposed that this stone was fashioned by some French sailors (possibly prisoners of war confined in Liverpool and on parole). This was the suggestion of old Captain Griffiths, aged eighty-five years, and an inmate of the Home for Aged Mariners. He recognised the stone and told Mr Kitchingman that he had played on it when quite a boy and called the game.

"Bumble puppy Stonehouse", writing in 1863, and describing the activities of the Pressgang about 1797, says:

"The men used to get across the water to Cheshire to hide until their ships were ready to sail. Near Egremont, on the shore, there used to be a little, low public-house known as Mother Redcap's, from the fact of the owner always wearing a red hood or cap. The public-house is still standing and I have often been in it. "and had their entire confidence. She had hiding places for any number. There is a tradition that the caves at the Red Noses communicated in some way and somewhere with Mother Redcap's. The men used, on returning from their voyages, to deposit communicated in some way and somewhere with Mother Redcap's. The men used, on returning from their voyages, to deposit with her their pay and prize money until they wanted it. It was known or at least very commonly believed that Mother Redcap good deal of prize money on their account, yet none of it was ever discovered. Some few years ago, I think about ten or twelve had in her possession enormous (for her) sums of money hidden or put away somewhere, but where that somewhere was, it was never known, for at her death very little property was found in her possession although only a few days before she died a rich prize was brought into Liverpool which yielded every sailor on board at least £1,000. Mother Redcap's was swarming with and many a strange story has been told and scene enacted under the old roof. "sailors belonging to the Privateer directly after the vessel had come into port, and it was known that the old lady had received a good deal of prize money on their account, yet none of it was ever discovered. Some few years ago, I think about ten or twelve (1850), a quantity of Spade Ace guineas was found in a cavity by the shore. It has always been a firm belief with me that someday a rich harvest will

be in store for somebody. Mother Redcap's was the resort of many a rough hard-hunted fellow, and many a strange story has been told and scene enacted under the old roof."

Smugglers and pirates were a real threat in the 1700's particularly to the Wallasey area, adored by both. They would often take wealthy residents and ransom them for money. There reputation also shows that they were also keen on kidnapping the poor and keeping them on board against their will to help out with labour on their vessel. This could also be said of the smugglers nemesis, the Royal Navy.

The Royal Navy notoriously picked up young and able men and recruited them into the ranks many times against their wishes, but the great terror of the sailors was the press other side of the Black Rock that they might conceal themselves in Cheshire, and many a vessel had to be brought into gang. Such was the dread in which this force was held by the sailors that they would often take to their boats on the port by a lot of riggers and carpenters sent round by the owners for that purpose."

Two entries in the Wallasey parish registers, both in 1762, refer to the risks the sailor ran. Under the date of 29th March, appears, ' William Evans drowned in endeavouring to escape from a cutter lying at ye Black Rock'; and again on 6th November, 'John Goss sailor drowned from ye Prince George tender in his Majesty's Service', the tender being the ship to which the men were sent immediately on being 'pressed.'

In his notes Mr Kitchingman says:

"Except in Mr Stonehouses Streets of Liverpool there does not seem to be any information to be obtained from writers about this spot. I can readily understand this as it was so out of the way and used for such secret purposes. I came on the scene and rooted it out for myself". In another place, he says: *"My father lodged at*
39

Mother Redcap's in 1820, and many of the notes of the old house here set out were made by him in that year".

Encamped on the Leasowes awaiting embarkation for Ireland. There is a tradition that at the time of King William's and a place from which pilots boarded vessels, besides being put to other uses. In 1690 the troops of William III were encamped on the Leasowes awaiting embarkation for Ireland. There is a tradition that at the time of King William's embarkation, dispatches were conveyed in a roundabout way to Chester, from Great Meols to Mother Redcap's, and then by fishing boats up the Mersey to Stoke and Stanney, instead of from Meols via Parkgate.

At an earlier period a small privateer called the Redcap cruised between here and Ireland. She took several dispatches for King James's partisans up to Stoke and Poole on the secluded upper reaches of the Mersey where some of the old Roman Catholic families resided.

Mr Coventry, a pilot well versed in Wallasey and Liscard folklore, stated that he had been told by his ancestors that several of King James's adherents, landed at Mother Redcap's. On one occasion three persons of some distinction were hurriedly landed from a ship. Horses were in readiness, and without a word the travellers rode off rapidly towards 'The Hooks'. Very soon afterwards a boat with an armed crew came from up river and made a hurried search. Mr Coventry said that the explanation his father heard at the time was that these refugees had made their escape from Ireland and were intending to proceed for refuge up the river towards Stoke or Stanney, but the tide being out, horses had been obtained here. The armed boat had been lying in wait higher up the river above Seacombe Point, and discovering the probability of a landing being made at Mother Redcap's, hurried down the river to intercept it.

The smuggling went on in this area for century's and storeys denote that on one occasion when the smugglers were desirous of getting a cask of rum or some other merchandise away from one of the hiding places, but were prevented by the unwelcome presence of a duty officer. So it was arranged that one of the smugglers was to creep down to the shore from the Moor, and lie down in his clothes in the water, at the edge of the receding tide. The attention of the solitary officer at Mother Redcap's was called to the supposed body which had been washed ashore, and he made his way to it as quickly as possible. He had removed the watch, and was going through the pockets when the corpse came to life, sprang up, and laid out the surprised officer with a swift blow from a melee weapon. By the time he had come to, the rum had been removed from Redcap's, and started its journey to the moss at Bidston.

No blame could be attached to the 'drowned man' who stated:

"He was walking along the shore, when he must have had a fit, for the next thing that he became aware of was that he was lying in the sand with his pockets being rifled. Thinking he was being robbed by a stranger he attacked". On another occasion a ship with tobacco on board was wrecked, and the watching officers saw two men run from the part of the wreck on the shore, along the beach northward, with two small bales as though they were about to depart for the Wallasey side. It took some time on the soft sand to overtake them, and when they were caught the packages were found to contain cabbage leaves and ferns. In the meantime their friends had made free with the real tobacco in the wreck.

Old Mr W. Whittle told Mr Kitchingman about 1896 that there was a great dispute concerning the right of way on the premises about 1750. It seems that when a dead body was found on the beach it was brought here and taken in by the back door. On removal for interment, on account of some superstition it was taken out by the

41

front door. Certain people claimed that if twelve bodies passed through in one year it gave a right of way for living people to pass through the house at any hour, day or night. An attempt was made once and once only, for a fierce fight ensued.

Whittle at one time had an idea of purchasing this cottage, but hearing this story which came from his wife's grandfather, he consulted Mr W. H. North, senior, about the legality of the supposed right of way; but Mr North only laughed at him. Doubtless the attempt referred to was a dodge on the part of the coastguard to obtain right of entry into the house. Mr W. Coventry once told Mr Kitchingman he believed Mother Redcap was a comely, fresh-coloured, Cheshire-spoken woman, and that she had at one time a niece to help her, who was very active but very offhand in her manners, and who afterwards married a Customs officer.

The first steam voyage across the Atlantic from Liverpool was made in the year 1838 by the City of Dublin Company's steamer Royal William, 617 tons, and 276 horse-powers. She left the Mersey on 5th July. A party of the Liverpool Dock trustees and ship owners assembled at Mother Redcap's to witness the departure, and a-cannon was fired from the front of the house as a farewell salute when the steamer passed on this side of the river to enter the Rock Channel. Mr J. Askew, the harbour-master, and Captain Dobie, of Messrs Brocklebank's ship Rimac, made speeches, and the belief was expressed that the vessel would not get beyond the Cove of Cork.

Mr J. Kitchingman was, it is said, born in the house in Withens Lane, lately the Horse and Saddle Inn. When he retired from Warrington, where he practised as a solicitor, he purchased and restored, in 1888, Mother Redcap's which had previously been a fisherman's cottage. He gave the land in front of it, when this portion of the promenade was made, on condition that it should not be used as a thoroughfare for carriages. When Royalty came to open a new addition to the Navy League Buildings, the royal and other carriages did drive along this part of the promenade, which so annoyed Mr Kitchingman that instead of leaving his house to the district, he left it instead to be used as a Convalescent Home for Warrington people, as his family belonged to that town. As it was not suitable for this purpose, the powers were obtained to set aside the will, and the property was sold. Mr Robert Myles became the purchaser, and he opened it as a café, bearing once more the name of Mother Redcap.

The small white cottage style tavern was demolished in 1885 and was rebuilt in 1888 in a mock Tudor style although it did continue being a public house. This is the taller building with spires which can be seen several old pictures that eventually became the café.

Unfortunately this building also demolished, this time in 1974 to make way for flats. Nothing now remains of Mother Red Caps except the solitary archway that marked the entrance, a bygone to a time of smuggling and maritime history.

The pathway in the next page, led from Wallasey Village to the Ring 'o Bells in Station Road Bidston, a smugglers route. There is a story about a customs man who, having been tipped off that there was to be a 'brandy run' across Bidston Moss, lay in wait for the smugglers. But they had found out about the tip off and substituted the brandy barrels for ordinary ale. They were stopped and obviously nothing was found! In the midst of the Moss was a bridge formed from whale bones, but eventually they sank into the marsh and vanished. All this area is now built on and Industry and Motorway now dominate. The railway line in the above image is the stem line from Seacombe Ferry to Bidston. The signal box is at the junction leading to Wallasey Village station.

Shipwreck

London Morning Post, Wednesday 8th November, 1820

On Wednesday night the brig Mary and Betty, *of this port, Thomas Lambert, master, burden 180 tons, with a cargo of corn, pigs, and sheep, on her voyage to Liverpool, was wrecked on the Ultarf, near*

Mockbegger.12 We are extremely concerned to add, that, of the crew and seven passengers, only three were saved. The Captain is among the number of those who perished.

Punishment For Plundering Of Wrecks

Jacksons Oxford Journal, Saturday 11th May, 1822

Thomas Moore, of Moreton, labourer, was convicted at the Chester Assizes of stealing ropes from the wreck of the Mary and Betty*, stranded on the Wallasey shore in October, 1820. and sentenced to death.13 It is hoped, that all those persons who have hitherto looked upon wrecking as a lawful trade, will learn from the sentence, that, by the law of the land, as well as the laws of humanity. It is considered a most atrocious crime. By the 26th of Geo.II. plundering a vessel in distress (whether wreck or no wreck) is felony without benefit of Clergy.*

Fortunatus Wright The Wallasey Privateer

Fortunatus Wright was the most famous British privateer commander and Liverpool's favourite hero during the first half of the eighteenth century. His exploits against the French during the War of Austrian Succession and later at the start of the Seven Years War would rival any adventure of Drake or Raleigh, and yet he is largely forgotten nowadays. He was a colourful mixture of rogue and swashbuckling hero, by all accounts a likeable villain.

We know that his father was a mariner – Captain John Wright – and that he died in 1717, because of a gravestone is in St. Peter's

---

12 London Morning Post, Wednesday 8th November, 1820

13 Jacksons Oxford Journal, Saturday 11th May, 1822

churchyard in Liverpool. The gravestone also records that the Captain "gallantly defended his ship for several hours against two vessels of superior force". We don't know very much about the early life of Fortunatus, except that he born in 1712 and became a brewer in Liverpool. We assume he learnt his sea-craft from his father.

In November 1732, at the age of 20, he married Martha Painter and had three daughters by her, including Phillipa who later married the grandson of the diarist, John Evelyn. Martha died a just a few years later. In November 1736, at the age of 24, he married Mary Bulkeley, who was already pregnant with his child.

War of Austrian Succession (1740 – 1748)

This ranged from 1740 until 1748, and throughout this time Letters of Marque were issued to merchants wishing to engage enemy shipping. We know that after marrying Mary Bulkely in 1736, FW went off to Italy and based himself there for the next twenty years or so, engaging in trade and later Privateering - financed by the merchants in the English 'colony' there.

Fortunatus Wright soon became a figure of controversy. In 1742 he was challenged at the gates of the city of Lucca (near Pisa in Northern Italy) and was ordered to give up his weapons. He refused and held a pistol to the head of one of the guards. Another 30 soldiers arrived and restrained him, and was arrested and held prisoner in his Inn for 3 days. Although he was eventually let off, he was forbidden to return. He moved to Leghorn.

Leghorn (or Livorno) is in Tuscany, a province of northern Italy. In the mid eighteenth century Austria was the dominant foreign power in Italy and Leghorn was supposedly a neutral port where merchants from all countries could trade and refit their vessels etc.

. . There was a large English 'colony' based in Leghorn, and it was these merchants that paid for the fitting out of a privateer vessel for Fortunatus Wright.

We should go back to 1746 and relate one last anecdote that is so typical of the character Fortunatus Wright was. A French vessel, double the size of FAME had been sent into Malta to hunt him down. Huge crowds of French sympathisers lined the coast as the two ships reappeared after a noisy and furious engagement. The French vessel was seen to be towing the badly damaged FAME, and as they rounded the headland the French flag was raised on the leading ship. A great cheer went up from the French - at last the scourge of the Mediterranean had been defeated. Suddenly, as the ships entered the harbour, the French flag was lowered and the British flag raised high above it – the French ship was in fact a prize to the British privateer, with its crew imprisoned in the hold and FW at the helm! On his father's tombstone in St.Peters' Church, Liverpool is included the following inscription: 'Fortunatus Wright, his son, was always victorious and humane to the vanquished. He was a constant terror to the enemies of his King and country.'

The Red & Yellow Noses

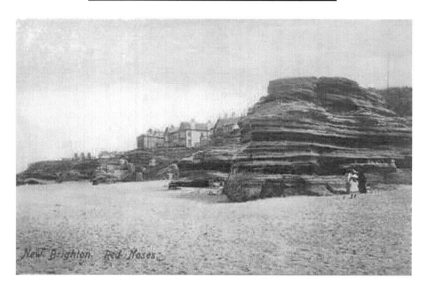

An outcrop of red sandstone known locally as the Red Noses, there are also yellow noses nearby. Here there are wide grassy area for camping and playing games and nearby a miniature golf course and tennis courts and at the other side of the railway Warren Park Golf Course and Harrison Park.

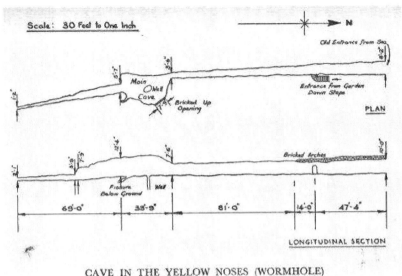

CAVE IN THE YELLOW NOSES (WORMHOLE)

The Red Noses are also famous for the involvement in pirating and smuggling in the 16th and 17th century, where people would hide in the Rocks and they lured ships onto the rocks and sandbanks at the mouth of the Mersey using lanterns on donkeys and beacons. The ships wrecked off Wallasey and New Brighton were then plundered and their cargoes stolen. Often sailors were drowned or murdered but that did not deter the wreckers.

New Brighton Begins

The Birth of New Brighton

James Atherton's prospectus, entitled 'Eligible Investment at New Brighton, Cheshire', stated that several gentlemen proposed to build a hotel and establish a ferry, to be called "The Royal Lighthouse Hotel and Ferry", which would have steam boats operating. The estimated cost would be £12,000, the sum to be raised by shares of £100 each.

The prospectus pointed out that views of the Welsh Mountains, Orme's Head and the Isle of Man could be seen from the site. It had "a beautiful beach" with hard clean sands. Villas were to be erected, together with a church, market place, shops, buildings, including a Post Office. The prospectus was dated October 1832 and the area was intended to attract the nobility and gentry rather than the working class.

Atherton's dream of every house having interrupted views of the sea began to take shape when a number of villas were built on

53

Wellington Road. His son-in-law, William Rowson, also played a huge part in the establishment of the new area.

Instead of keeping the name of Rock Point, they decided to call the new district a new name. It was to be like Brighton in the south of England, so this became "New" Brighton. Within a short period of time New Brighton went from a small fishing hamlet to a complete new town with a population of some 6,000 by 1880. It was the popularity of trains and ferries that would see New Brighton become a popular resort.

James Atherton

The man who shaped New Brighton

James Atherton was born at Ditton near Widnes, in 1770. Born to William and Margaret Atherton, James was the eighth of ten children, six boys and four girls. His father William (1732-1807) was a yeoman farmer and from the time of his marriages to James' mother, at the adjoining village of Farnworth in 1755, William spent most of his life occupied in husbandry at Ditton. Margaret, too, came from farming stock and her father, Thomas Houghton, was a yeoman farmer at nearby Prescot.

Little is known of James Atherton's early life and education. However, with a large household and no great wealth in the family - his father left a moderate £800 in his will - it seems probable that James spent his adolescence on the farm at Ditton with his siblings. There was certainly little future prospect for him as a farmer, being the youngest of William's six sons. Thus, it seems probable that James had made the short journey to Liverpool by the time he reached his early-twenties.

The most positive reference to James Atherton's early life occurs in September 1792 when he married Betty Rowson at Grappenhall Parish Church, near Warrington. This indisputable record gives us the clearest indication yet that he had already been drawn to the thriving port of Liverpool, as details from the marriage licence confirm his association with the town and also give his occupation, which is recorded as a 'grocer'. Gore's Directory for the year 1796 places this early venture in the heart of the old town at Pool Lane (later South Castle Street) and the same source verifies Atherton's occupation. The newlyweds appeared to settle quickly in Pool Lane and their first child, a daughter named Mary, was baptised at St Nicholas Church, Chapel Street, Liverpool, just over one year later in October 1793. By 1798, James and Betty had produced two more daughters, Margaret, born in 1795, and Eliza, born in 1797. The business, too, seems to have been quite successful as the following year the young family moved a short distance away to more spacious premises in Dale Street where, in the same year, Betty gave birth to a fourth child; a son, christened James after his father.

In keeping with the common practice of most businesses in the eighteenth century, Atherton, who was by now describing himself a merchant, 'lived on the job', and he fixed a link with these Dale Street promises which, in purely professional terms, he was to maintain for the remainder of his life. In addition, it was also about this time that Atherton is believed to have become more closely involved in the overseas trade. According to R.F Mould in his book 'The Iron Church' - which promotes a short history of St George's Church, Everton - Atherton was an active shareholder in shipping companies, and was also said to have flirted with the slave trade by purchasing a principals share in a slave ship by the name of 'Irene'.

However, there appears to be very little evidence available to support the latter claim. James Atherton's name does not appear upon the 'Lists of the Company of Merchants trading to Africa' for the late eighteenth and/or early nineteenth century for instance, while, it is also worth remembering, that the propensity to associate almost every merchant in eighteenth century Liverpool with the vile trade in human cargo can sometimes be rather unfairly exaggerated. Another Atherton, John Atherton is listed, yet he appears to be unrelated to James. Still, exclusion from these records does not necessarily prove or disprove James Atherton's possible connection with slavery. As Cameron and Crooke's 'Liverpool - Capital of the Slave Trade' publication have rightly indicated, slave trading ventures were usually organised by a partnership of between two and a dozen more individuals. Similarly, 'sleeping partners', whose involvement was limited to the investment of some of the finance and a corresponding share of the profit, could easily disguise their interest. Suffice to say, therefore, that James Atherton's involvement remains uncertain. What is certain that the Parliamentary Bill for the Abolition of Slavery received Royal Assent in March, 1837, and whatever the extent of his former mercantile activities, by that date James Atherton was preoccupied with concentrating most of his efforts towards the development of land and property at the western-end of Everton village.

At the beginning of the nineteenth century, the population of Liverpool was continuing upon its upward spiral at a quite alarming rate and, thus, James and Betty Atherton's attention was directed towards the desirable prospect of Everton for the first time. A contemporary description of Everton Village from the year 1800 gives an indication of the scene to which the family aspired.

"A pretty village with a view which embraces town, village, plain, pasture and river. At sunset the windows of the houses of Everton Brow flash back the glowing radiance showing that nothing impedes the wide prospect westwards"

Hence, James Atherton departed the city in 1803 and removed his growing family to Everton Village. The move coincided with the birth of the Atherton's second son, William. Four more children, Charles (b.1808); Caroline (b.1809); Henry Regent (b.1811); and George, (b.1815) followed within the next twelve years to complete the family. At the time of his move to Everton, Atherton was thirty-three years old. It would prove to be a crucial transitional period when the former farmers-boy, grocer and merchant entered into the razor-sharp competitiveness of land and property dealing.

Initially, Atherton purchased a large tract of land belonging to the St Domingo Estate. He then built his own house on the high ground near to the old Everton Beacon, and commenced with the lay-out of a new street close by. A contemporary of Atherton's, Robert Syers, had described in his book, 'A History of Everton', published in 1830, of the erection of "several handsome mansions and delightful villas' in this street, which Atherton called 'Albion Crescent', a name he would later reproduce in one of New Brighton's first streets. These houses were snapped up by men of a similar ilk to Atherton. Leading merchants, who had compatible social aspirations and who were equally determined to desert the restrictive and unhealthy conditions predominating in the city centre.

The success of Albion Crescent enabled Atherton to lay-out further new streets on his land such as; Northumberland Terrace, York Terrace and Grecian Terrace. These particular street names still survive in Everton today, albeit with vastly different types of property to those of Atherton's day. The pinnacle of this development was St George's Church. Designed by the architect Thomas Rickman, and built by John Clegg on the years 1912-1814 on land donated by Atherton. R.F Mould, in his history of St George's, records that the sum of £11,500 was necessary to build the church. This was obtained by the issue of 115 shares of £100 each, with no shareholder allowed to purchase more than ten shares and James Atherton was one of only two people to purchase a maximum quota of ten shares.

Atherton's own house was situated directly opposite St George's in Northumberland Terrace and the family continued to reside in this house until their move to New Brighton in the early 1830s. Mould goes on to provide a very interesting account of the proximity of these two buildings which vividly portrays Atherton's significant influence in Everton at the time. As a condition of the land he donated, Atherton stipulated that...

"...no funerals at the church or persons attending them shall enter or retire through the western gale of the churchyard without express permission of James Atherton or his heirs"

And this provision was duly incorporated into the 1813 St George's Church Act of Parliament.

By 1823, Atherton had officially retired from business at the age of fifty-three; He had acquired 'gentleman' status and, in the process, had become a very wealthy man. His achievements during the previous thirty years, from the modest start of the grocer's shop in

59

Pool Lane, had been impressive by any standards and were marked by what J.A. Picton described Atherton in his 'Memorials of Liverpool, published in 1903, as an 'ardent, bold and daring character ...everything he undertook was carried out on a scale of magnificence being always occupied with a variety of schemes for improvement and progress'. On a similar note, Syers described Atherton as 'a man in ten thousand...it may truly be said of him that he was born to be busy'.

It is from such accounts of Atherton's character that one began to understand why his retirement was so short lived. In 1830, James Atherton, in association with his son-in-law William Rowson, began negotiations with John Penkett, Lord of the Manor of Liscard to buy a large section of land at the north-eastern end of the Township.14

Effectively, his successful development of Everton represented a blueprint of his subsequent plans for New Brighton, albeit on a smaller scale. When Atherton left Everton village it was being described in the following terms;

"Everton now abounds with handsomely walled pleasure grounds and well-enclosed fields, and is conveniently intersected with admirable roads, most of them well-paved, and many of the parapets are flagged for two-thirds of their breadth with admirable well laid strong flags".

The village's population had increased almost ten-fold since James Atherton's arrival. He was a highly respected member of the local community and a pillar of the church, he was wealthy enough to sit back and enjoy his retirement in comfort, yet at the age of sixty, he was prepared to take a major chance and speculate in a new and

<hr>

14 Almost An Island, Noel E. Smith

much larger project in the "wilds" of Cheshire. One considers what went through the mind when he made his decision.

Character references have shown that Atherton was an astute businessman with an eye for profit, and the land adjoining the Black Rock had enormous potential. But there may have been less tangible reasons behind his reasons. Firstly, Everton was beginning to experience the first signs of an encroachment from the city centre. The growth which had engulfed the old town a generation earlier had begun to reach the Townships away from the river. Ultimately, Everton's distinct individuality would be swallowed up by a tide of terraced housing advancing up the slopes to the village. Secondly, there is evidence of a more profound nature. The last decade of Atherton's tenancy at Everton was clouded by personal tragedy. James and Betty lost three sons, James Junior, Charles and Henry Regent. All within just a few years age of each other, at the ages of nineteen, twenty-one and twenty respectively. The death of a child is particularly hard to bear for parents, but their sons' individual deaths, at such young ages, must have been devastating for them both. In such circumstances, Everton may have held too many painful memories for the family. Taken separately, these events may not have been enough to influence Atherton's decision, yet put together there seems a very strong possibility that they precipitated the move to New Brighton.

On 24th January 1832, William Rowson advanced a deposit of £200 to John Penkett on account of the purchase of the "New Brighton Estate". The sum represented £100 each for himself and James Atherton.

A fresh start and a new challenge lay ahead for the two men but before the main plans were laid James Atherton died in 1838. Before his death he chose to be buried back at St George's church with his children James, Charles, and Henry who died before him.

His wife, daughter Caroline and family plus others are also buried there.15

New Brighton Fort Perch Rock

During the early 1800's the various merchants and others of the area thought the Port of Liverpool should be guarded and when the old Perch Rock Light was washed away the authorities thought of the idea of having a fortified lighthouse, or having a fort which would contain a lighthouse. It was finally agreed to have two separate constructions at a meeting held on 25th March 1825. The fort covers about 4,000 square yards and is constructed of mainly red sandstone which came largely from the Runcorn Quarries; it was floated down the Mersey and unloaded when the tide was out. Because the stone was soft it had to be left to be weathered.

The walls were originally 24 feet and 29 feet high, but these, in some cases, were heightened to almost 32 feet, facing the river side and the towers 40 feet high. The fort had a slipway with three arches with drawbridge and a Tuscan portal bearing the Coat of

15 The Inviting Shore, Anthony M. Miller

Arms and the words "Fort Perch Rock". It was cut off at high tides from the mainland. The fort built on what was known as Black Rock, stood guard at the mouth of the river, shipping passing 950 yards from the battery. The fort was armed with eighteen guns, of which sixteen were 32 pounders, mounted on platforms. Six were placed on the west front, two on the east and four on the north. Single guns were placed in the towers and along the angles. There were two small guns facing the causeway. There was accommodation for 100 men, with officers' quarters and kitchen. There were also storerooms and Magazine in the centre of the courtyard at a sunken level, with a hand-hoist for lifting the ammunition.

Perch Rock Battery, New Brighton.   www.tonyfranks-buckley.com

In the early years, the guns were smooth-bore cannon and the balls had to be heated in a furnace until they were red hot, and then shipped to the guns for firing. The idea being when they scored a direct hit they would set the enemy ship alight and set off their powder. The fort would have a practice from time to time, when the local fishermen would gather the cannon balls and return them to the fort, receiving payment for them. The fort was nicknamed the "Little Gibraltar of the Mersey".

As the Rock Channel slowly became silted, the larger ships ceased to use it and it became necessary to equip the battery with larger guns capable of reaching the range. 64 pounders were installed as a result and these were mounted in granite. The old 32 pounders were kept to guard the Rock Channel which was still being used by the smaller ships. The 4th Cheshire Company o Artillery Volunteers was established after holding an open meeting, to set up a local corp. On the 31st January, 1860 the New Brighton Company was started and it was not long before they had 60 men under the command of Captain Henry D. Grey and his staff. Their uniform was dark blue with white facings and in full dress they wore a Busby.

At a later date, the corps became known as the 1st Cheshire and Caernarvon Artillery then, soon after the turn of the century, they joined with the 1st Lancashire Artillery Volunteers, forming the Lancashire and Cheshire Heavy Brigade. The M.O. at the Fort was Dr. J. W. Lloyd whose son, Selwin, became Foreign Secretary. In the Second World War the unit became the "420 Coast Regiment", until they were disbanded in November, 1960.

When the Royal Artillery was stationed at the fort, there were three officers and 101 men. In 1943 there were two officers and 28 men, and finally one officer and 8 men, as a maintenance unit in April

1944. After the war, it had one officer, one master-gunner and two other ranks. Whilst the territorial's were there, they had one officer and 28 men. The Home Guard also had a spell there.

The fort controlled the Mersey Division Submarine Miners in the late 1800's. They used to lay mines both at sea and on land. Some of the men employed in the task were members of the Wallasey Ferries. In 1893 the battery was dismantled and the guns returned to Ordnance, the following year two 4.7" Quick Firing guns were delivered but due to a change of plans, as regards a second fort being built, they were installed at Seaforth Battery on the opposite side of the river. Perch Rock was to have three 6" guns installed. At the same time the Royal Engineers took over the fort and re-modelling was commenced.

The parade yard was no longer needed, as the infantry had left in 1858. It was partly filled in with sand and rocks from the beach and covered. The pits were constructed for the naval guns, which were mounted away from the walls and these were lowered so the guns could have a close range of 150 yards, Electricity was available from a new engine-room. The maximum machine guns at the fort were installed in May 1893. The 6" guns arrived in December 1897, but it was not until March 1899 that they were fully installed and ready for action. Some ten years later, between 1909 and 1910, further alterations were carried out and Mark VII guns were installed. When these were brought to the Fort, the drawbridge was strengthened to allow for the extra load. Over the next few years, search-light towers and an observation tower were built.

At the outbreak of the First World War, the war office decided to remove two of the 6" guns, one of which was later returned in 1923. Finally the armament of the fort was two 6" guns and two machine-guns, which remained until 1954. The drawbridge was removed in 1935.The modern concrete tower was used to house the Radar which was added in 1941, but this was not the only modern invention at the fort for, as early as 1895, the range-finder system operated with a lens in either tower. They could determine the distance, in a way similar to that in a non-reflex miniature camera. During the Second World War, the fort was made to appear as a sort of tea-garden from the air. The letters TEAS were painted on the roof of one of the buildings and the outer portion was painted green, to give the effect of a lawn.

In War time the fort went into action only twice in its entire history. The first was on the outbreak of the First World War, when a round was fired across the bow of an approaching Norwegian ship under sail, which failed to obey a signal from the fort. It was at the time when the Territorial's were at the fort, under the command of Major Charles Luga, who was a local dentist. He ordered a warning shot, which was way off the mark, as the gun was elevated too much. It landed in Crosby on the opposite side of the mouth of the river. They fired again, only to hit the bow of an Allen Liner at anchor! The first shell landed in the sand hills and was found by a resident, who took it to the Seaforth Battery, where the officer placed it in the Mess Room, with the words "A present from New Brighton". The Captain of the Norwegian ship thought they were just having a bit of fun. He did not know that War had been declared.

The second occasion the fort went into action was again on the outbreak of war, on September 1939, a fishing-smack came up the Rock channel which had been closed. Colonel Charles Cocks the Battery Commander ordered two shots to be fired across her bows from No. 2 gun. The owner of the fishing-smack was ordered to pay £25 for each round. The fort was dismantled in 1954, a caretaker appointed and 1958 it was put up for sale, having been offered to both Liverpool and Wallasey Corporations. It was sold by auction in 1958 for £4000. It was used for a number of years as a sort of pleasure centre, but the council objected and after the storms of 1975, it was again put on the market, the next owner with the help of the Manpower Services Commission, restored it to something like its original 1826 design, removing tons of sand from the old parade ground, and made the Magazine into a museum of the War Plane Wreck Investigation Group.

The New Brighton Artillery Volunteers

Liverpool Mercury, Monday 27th August, 1860

The 4th Cheshire (New Brighton) artillery volunteers commenced firing practice on Saturday afternoon last, at the Rock Perch Battery, and the 5th Cheshire (Birkenhead) artillery corps, under the command of Captain Laird, attended by invitation to witness the firing of their comrades in arms, by whom they were afterwards hospitality entertained.16 Five rounds of blank cartridges were fired, namely, two rounds with intervals of three-quarters of a minute, one with intervals of ten seconds, one with intervals of eight seconds, and one with intervals of about two

---

16 Liverpool Mercury, Monday 27th August, 1860

seconds, and the manner in which the guns were handled called forth the admiration of the regular artillerymen in charge of the fort. The spectators included a large number of ladies and gentlemen living at New Brighton and in the neighbourhood, for whose gratification the band of the 5th performed several pieces of music during the evening.

Perch Rock Lighthouse

Perch Rock, New Brighton Lighthouse, sits next to the fort, it was originally, a wooden "Perch", hence its name. A large post held a light on top and was supported by a sort of tripod. It was erected on the Black Rock in 1683 by the Liverpool Corporation. When foreign ships, passed the old perch, they were charged sixpence for its respect and to keep it in repair. But it was often washed away and a boat had to be launched to recover it from Bootle Bay. In February 1821, the pilot boat "Liver" crashed into the perch and carried it away. It has been said that it was washed away in March 1824 and not recovered until the December. However the cost of replacing it all the time grew too expensive and it was decided to build a new one.

The foundation stone of the new lighthouse was laid on 8th June 1827 by Thomas Littledale, Mayor of Liverpool. It was designed on the lines of Eddy stone by Mr. Foster and built of marble rock from Anglesey by Tomkinson & Company. It rises 90 feet above the rocks and is considered to be a masterpiece of craftsmanship.

The granite cost 1/6d a cubic foot. Each piece of stone is interlocked into the next. The whole stonework, when finished, was coated with what is known as "Puzzellani" a volcanic substance from Mount Etna which, with age, becomes rock hard. The first 45 feet is solid. A spiral staircase leads to where the keeper lived and then on to the lantern house. The revolving light was said to be the first in the country. It cost £27,500 to construct.

Work was only possible at low tide and it was not completed until 1830. Its first light shone on the 1st March of that year and consisted of two white flashes, followed by one red, with a range of 14 miles. The light was 77 feet above the half-tide level. It was eventually electrically connected to the mainland.

Liverpool Mercury, 20th November 1870

Inquest at New Brighton

An inquest was held yesterday at New Brighton, by Mr.Churton, coroner, on the body of John Green, aged 50, keeper of the Rock lighthouse, New Brighton.17 It appeared that the unfortunate man, about ten o'clock on Monday night last ascended the ladder for the purpose of examining the light. About ten minutes afterwards he was found lying insensible on the balcony by his assistant. He was at once conveyed to his home at New Brighton, and Dr. Mushet was called in, but he died on the following day. A verdict of "Accidental death" was returned.

The Lighthouse last shone its light on 1st October 1973 as it was no longer needed on account of the radar system operating in the river. A local architect purchased the lighthouse for £100 on condition he maintained the construction, he tried to restore the lantern again but the river authorities thought it might cause confusion to local shipping. So he refurbished it so that anyone could stay there for a short holiday. Indeed, it was their idea to attract newly married couples to spend part of their honeymoon there at a cost of £50 a day, with champagne and flowers thrown

---

17 Liverpool Mercury, 20th November 1870

in. With electricity being introduced, the old lighthouse has a galley with cooker and refrigerator and, on the first floor, a bathroom with shower. There is a living room and a bedroom on the next two floors. The lighthouse even has a television, just in case one gets bored with looking at the sea. A ladder has to be obtained from the fort to gain the necessary height to reach the 15 iron rungs of the lighthouse as the door is 25 feet from the base.

The Liscard Battery of New Brighton

In the 1750's, The Corporation of Liverpool decided to move the Powder Magazines, used to store explosive and shot from ships in port, from their site in Clarence Street and find a more isolated site for them on the Cheshire side of the River Mersey. Accordingly, a suitable plot was purchased on the south bank of the Mersey at Wallasey and the new magazine constructed. They were renovated and enlarged in 1838-39, and were still in use until 1851, when it was decided that in future explosives would be stored in hulks further up the river at the Bight of Sloyne. The move was probably prompted by safety concerns, the land around the Magazines having become much more built up. In 1858 a battery was built on the site, and the imposing gateway with its crenulated towers, survives to this day as does the perimeter wall which now encircles several houses. Facing the south wall of the battery, on the other side of the road (Magazine Brow) are several cottages, perhaps dating from the 17th Century. These were probably first inhabited by fishermen, but it is thought that they were later occupied by offices from the battery.

The Magazines were often referred to as Liscard Magazines and the fort as Liscard Battery, but the name Liscard later became attached to an area about a mile away where Wallasey's main shopping area is situated. A quaint circular dwelling may be seen about fifty yards from the fort's gateway, this being known as the Round House. Now forming part of a private residence, this was once occupied by the battery's watchman. Further along Magazine

Brow are situated two public houses, the Pilot Boat and The Magazines, the latter having been built in 1759 and once used by sailors who were having their outward bound ships reloaded with munitions at the Liscard Magazines.

This impressive structure which is still partially standing is one of the great land marks of the area. Nestled between Magazine Lane and Magazine Brow, the old structure kept watch across the River Mersey as an additional line of defence against all manner of seaborne threats. Britain was just coming out of the Indian colonies mutiny and was strengthening it defensive positions especially for the supply lines of shipping.

The River Mersey was already protected by Fort Perch rock but it was decided to build another structure which could train its guns on all vessels within the Mersey. A spot at the river's edge in New Brighton was selected. The area was just opposite the now dismantled powder magazines. Work began in 1858 on the project and the large fort was completed built from locally quarried heavy red sand stone. The fort was an impressive defensive structure capable of holding seven 10 inch guns and a small detachment of the 55th Royal Artillery.

Magazine Brow with Liscard Battery, Wallasey, Wirral - by Harold Hopps

In those days the gunners of the fort would have wore a smart navy blue frock as opposed to a full dress tunic. Each of the uniforms had a red stripe down the leg complete with brass buttons and smart black shoes. The officers of the time would have worn a white belt and sash. When the fort was first constructed the men's head wear would have consisted of fur Busby hats. This was later replaced in 1878 with a blue-cloth covered helmet complete with spike, which was again replaced in 1881 with a ball.

The forts most cunning feature was not nits, thick walls or heavy artillery, buts simply its location. The fort stood at the water's edge slightly set back, but completely hidden by a variety of foliage. From the river, the fort was not visible until it was too late and by that time it would be within firing distance. This earned the Liscard Battery the nick name of *"The Snake in the Grass"*. Fortunately for the local residents the fort was never fired against by any enemies and as time drew on the fort became obsolete without conflict. In 1912 the fort was sold to the Liverpool Yacht Club and over the years it had fallen into a sorry state of repair resulting in its demise. In addition to this many houses now occupy the site, both inside and outside of the forts walls as the photo above describes. The houses opposite the fort still stand and they also play a part in the history of the Liscard Battery. The officers from the fort lived opposite in the red sandstone house. Many of the houses along the road are extremely old, one even dating to 1747. The outline of the Battery is still visible today and is one of the many remaining features of Wallasey's past.

NEW BATTERY ON THE CHESHIRE COAST

Cheshire Observer, Saturday, 10th March, 1860

Whilst there is so much talk about the defences of the port, it is not a little singular that that no notice has been taken publicly of the construction of a small but very powerful battery on the sea coast of Liscard just completed, immediately below the site of the old Powder Magazine. This may arise from the fact that the battery, which is en barbette, is semi-masked in character; and the passengers to New Brighton by the boats see nothing but a plain wall and innocent grass mound where there are placed in position, under proper protection and in working order, seven of the largest sized guns in her majesty's service, and whose concentrated fire would sink the largest ship afloat. The works which have been very quietly conducted, have been two years in progress; but the armament has only recently been completed, -- about twenty of the militia artillery from Liverpool being taken over to assist in the mounting of the monster guns. The Liscard Battery, which can in no sense be called a fortress, is, however, enclosed by a substantial stone wall, quadrangular in form, of no great thickness or height, but with a low tower at three of the corners, and one at each side of the gateway. The wall, which is of red mended, and there is a small window or look-out in each of the towers. There is barrack accommodation inside – and not of the most superior description – for about 30 gunners; but the place of course, will never be fully occupied except in case of positive danger. A winding earthen parapet parapet serves as a shelter for the guns, which are placed on two tiers of different elevation, four on the upper and three on the lower.

Some idea of the size of the guns may perhaps be formed from the fact that they weigh about 88 cwt. each, and that they are ten inches in diameter at the mouth of the bore. They are also of considerable length, being in fact rather long howitzers than guns. Like most other ordnance for coast, river, or harbour defences, they are intended for shells, grape, and canister, rather than solid shot. They are of size sufficient for the projection of a hollow shot weighing 87½ lbs. The guns are mounted on traversing platforms, which describe sufficient of a circle to admit of the whole of them being brought to bear upon one object; and the power of concentrating the fire, added to the size of the guns, gives to this small and otherwise insignificant work, a character really formidable.18 The North Fort, which lies almost immediately opposite on the Liverpool side, is quite commanded by this battery. It certainly mounts more guns, but they are of less calibre; they could only be concentrated to a very limited extent in this particular direction, two guns at the most being brought to bear; whilst the whole seven of the Liscard battery could rain destruction upon the North Fort. This being so, the startling thought naturally arises, that there is nothing to prevent a battery, which could inflict such damage on Liverpool side, from being taken in the rear. In case of hostile invasion, a land force would be absolutely necessary for its protection; and certainly commodious barracks could be found in the old Magazines immediately above, which appear now to serve the use only of barns to a neighbouring farmer. This Liscard battery is completely furnished with stores, comprising the latest form of shell, and every new mechanical appliance; and, waiting only the complement of gunners, who could be speedily brought from Chester, it is ready for action at a minute's notice.

---

18 Cheshire Observer, Saturday, 10th March, 1860

On dit that the Rock or Perch will shortly pulled down, and a new battery en barbette constructed in its stead, and that abandoning the idea of the north shore at Liverpool as unsuitable in many respects, the military authorities have been surveying various sites on the Birkenhead side, to find a suitable open, where the artillery volunteers of the district may be exercised in throwing up earthworks and practicing their guns.

New Brighton Promenade

Magazine Promenade. New Brighton.

Until 1891, the river front was open to the shore. The only built up are as being the Ferries. If a traveller on the river prior to this period looked toward Wallasey he would have seen mainly eroded clay cliffs supported by a large masonry wall (1858-1863). It was impossible to pass directly from Seacombe to Egremont via this route. At the Guinea Gap there was an actual hole in the cliff in which the tide had carved out a large hollow. From Egremont to what is now New Brighton, existed only private properties occupying the foreshore.

THE PROMENADE, FLORAL PAVILION AND BATTERY, NEW BRIGHTON www.tonyfranks-buckley.com

www.tonyfranks-buckley.com

The Seacombe - New Brighton promenade was completed in stages, to 1901. New Brighton Ferry started in 1906. In 1931 work started on building a seawall to Harrison Drive, Wallasey Village, even by today's standards, an ambitious project. Included in the project would be an embankment 130 feet wide, 46 acres of public gardens, a marine lake (for model boats), open air bathing and subsequent roadways. With the exception of the public gardens, it was completed in 1939.

The land between the railway and the promenade was left untouched due to the arrival of WW2. In fact nothing was done to this area at all until the 1990s when developers got their greedy mitts on it and built "luxury apartments". More revenue for the council and no lay out in costs! The Home Guard (Dad's Army) were located at their HQ in the School of Art. In fact some of the guard were enlisted as students too!!

Brickworks Dispute on the Promenade

Liverpool Mercury, 7th December 1877

Works and Health Committee

The committee had been in communication with the Wallasey Brick and Land Company with reference to the closing of the foot road between Egremont ferry and Manor Road slip by the company19.

---

19 Liverpool Mercury, 7th December 1877

No terms had been come to, and it was recommended that the opinion of Mr. North, solicitor, should be taken on the subject.

Liverpool Mercury, 8th December 1877

A brick making company, whose workers are situated between the Egremont Ferry and the manor slip, having stopped the footway adjoining the sea wall, the Wallasey Local Board have apparently determined on vindicating the public rights, and on Thursday night, between six and seven o'clock, the obstruction was removed by them. Yesterday morning the brick making company re-erected the barrier, which was again pulled down yesterday afternoon on the authority of the local board. It is stated that on both occasions the services of the Wallasey fire brigade were called into requisition, and, having laid the hose along the wall, with a full pressure of water on, they were prepared, if necessary, to meet with a plentiful supply of cold water any attempt interfere with the performance of their duty. We understand that no resistance was made. The attempted obstruction has excited considerably feeling in the locality, and great satisfaction is expressed at the prompt and vigorous action of the authorities.20

Liverpool Mercury, 10th December 1877

The stupid and dangerous course adopted by the brick making company of Egremont in opposing by force the determination of the authorities to keep open the roadway abutting the sea wall north of the ferry resulted in a great popular demonstration on Saturday, accompanied by scenes which raised the liveliest apprehensions of a formidable riot.

---

20 Liverpool Mercury, 8th December 1877

On Thursday and Friday last the company erected barricades across the roadway, and these, as previously reported, were removed by the authorities. During Friday night, however, the company constructed two formidable barricades, protected by trenches filled with water, and made other preparations which unmistakeably indicated that active resistance would be made to any attack upon them. The likelihood of a "row" caused an immense gathering of people in the neighbourhood early in the afternoon, and the number received large accessions as the fire brigade – in brass helmets and carrying their usual implements – mustered in the vicinity of the ferry between two and three o'clock. At this time Inspector Hindley and a body of fine stalwart policemen; while among the crowd were officials and several members of the local board.

Some formal requests to remove the barrier having been made to the brickmakers and refused, the storming party of firemen gallantly rushed to their task, and vigorously assailed the first barricade with axes and levers. What with the trench and the state of the outworks, inches deep in a claysy puddle – their task was no easy or pleasant one, and it was soon rendered much more difficult and unpleasant by hissing jets of steam from pipes connected with the boilers in the brickworks, which were brought to play upon them. The firemen's response was cold water from the hose in sufficient quantity and force to speedily confound the enemy's politics; and though enveloped in steam they could be seen now and then plying axe and lever with the utmost vigour, despite numberless unfriendly attentions from the brickmen behind the palisadings. While this excellent public service was being done, some persons inside the works thought it a good joke to utilise the bricks which lay plentifully about them, and a shower of these dangerous missiles were directed against the attacking party. Amongst these were many person who, unfortunately, did not wear helmets, and they speedily betook themselves to a safe distance. At this critical juncture the police interfered with admirable promptness, and having "spotted" three or four of the men inside the works in the act of throwing the bricks, rushed in upon them and made them prisoners. This action, together with the intimation that such of the directors or shareholders who were egging the workmen on would, if they persisted, be dealt with in the same manner, as inciting to a breach of the peace, at once out a stop to the brick-throwing; and the upshot was the complete and speedy demolition of the barricades, amidst great cheering.21 The appearance of many of the besiegers and defenders, covered with clay from head to foot, was a sight not to be forgotten. Our reporter hears that the workmen arrested were taken to the lockup, and subsequently bailed out. Of course the affair caused intense excitement, and the brick throwing incident aroused loud cries of indignation, which might have easily resulted in serious damage of property, if not to limb, for there were hundreds of sturdy fellows who were ready, if necessary, to storm the works as well as the barricades, and give the instigators of the obstruction a thorough ducking.

All through Saturday night and yesterday a force was kept ready for immediate action should another endeavour be made to stop the road.

Liverpool Mercury, 13th December 1877

Magisterial Compliment to the Police

At the Wallasey petty sessions yesterday, before Messrs Chambres (chairman), Penny, Bouch, Kerford, Mann, and Bulley, the three men in the employ of the Wallasey Brick and Land Company who, as already reported, were taken into custody for participation in a riot at Egremont on the 6th instant, appeared to their

---

21 Liverpool Mercury, 10th December 1877

recognisances. Their names are Charles Loder (manager of the company), John Fishwick and Patrick Boyd (labourers), all charged with riotous conduct, and the last named with assaulting Police Constable 162. Mr Wright, of the firm, Wright, Stockley and Becket, appeared for the accused.

From the full particulars of the occurrence which were published in the Mercury, it will be remembered that on Saturday afternoon, the 8th instant, an effort was made by the Wallasey Brick and Land Company to close to the public a piece of land about eight yards wide, running along the river wall on the Cheshire side from Egremont Ferry Pier to Manor Road or Maddocks slip, which had been used for many years as a footpath between the places named. The company had recently purchased the land in question, and it was owing to their exercising proprietary rights that the public interfered. On Thursday last the company erected a barricade to prevent the public walking along the river wall, but that night it was removed by someone opposed to its existence. A similar barrier was erected on the following day, but a similar fate awaited it, and it was removed that afternoon. In neither of these cases was there any disturbance or opposition. On Saturday, however, the barricade had been again erected by the company and more ingenious appliances brought to bear against its demolition. About three o'clock p.m. on that day another attempt was made to clear the obstruction, the Wallasey fire brigade under Mr. Leather, lending their assistance. A crowd of about 4000 persons collected, and somewhat dangerous proceedings ensued. Fortified with large hammers, picks, &c, the members of the fire brigade commenced the work of pulling down the barrier, but were compelled to desist for a time by the company's employees turning on steam from the works some distance behind into perforated iron tubes which had been placed on either side of the barricade. The police came upon the scene just in time to prevent a more serious disturbance, but, as it was, several stones and brickbats were thrown by men in the company's yard as well as by their opponents on the river wall.

The first witness now called was Inspector Hindley, of the Cheshire County Police, who deposed in the main to the facts as already published. When he saw the affair was getting serious, he ordered the policemen present to take anyone into custody who threw stones. Two of the men in custody, Boyd and Loder, were on the company's fence directing the steam from two tubes upon the people on the river wall. Witness handcuffed and took into custody the manger of the company (Loder). Police Constables 147, 162, 157, and 165 all gave corroborative evidence.

Mr. Wright submitted that the magistrates had no jurisdiction in the matter, inasmuch as it was purely a question of title to land. An action would forthwith be brought by the company against those who were the instigators of the occurrence, and he would like to say a few words to convince the bench that the company have exclusive rights over the whole of the land referred to. Mr. Wright then went on to explain that the company, early in the present year, bought the land in question, and by the agreement entered into were to pay for every yard of it, including the portion in dispute. The men from whom they purchased it claimed the freehold and fee simple of every portion of the land without the reservation of any right of way whatever. The company erected their works in due course close to the river wall without any desire to prevent the public walking along the strip of land to and from Egremont Ferry. The lapse of time, however, without any interference would give the public a right of way, and as the bench would be aware, for 18 or 20 years the wall had been there. If for 20 years the public had used the passage without the company asserting its rights, a right of way would be established there, and what they considered a most valuable part of their property – namely the river frontage for shipping bricks – would lapse from them. It was only after very mature deliberation that the company had come to the conclusion to assert its right, and they only intended to keep the passage closed for a day or two. The company offered the local board some time ago £2000 worth of land if they (the board) would construct a road 10 yards broad along the river frontage, reserving to the company the right to use it as they otherwise would be entitled to use it for their tramways upon lines level with the road. The local board, however, refused to accept the offer. Subsequently due notice was given to the public that the road would be closed, and as it was their only course, the company erected the barricades, with the result already known. The steam pipe referred to was not concealed at all, and notice was given before the steam was turned on. In conclusion, Mr. Wright quoted from Okes' Magisterial Synopsis, section 46, to show that the bench had no jurisdiction in the matter.

The Chairman said the magistrates thought they had jurisdiction in a case of riot like the present, but they would retire and consult their law advisor.

After a few minutes' consultation the magistrates returned into court, and, having taken their seats, Mr. Chambres, addressing Mr. Wright, said that they understood that the brick company contemplated building another barricade. Stronger than those which has been built, and they wanted to ask if there was any truth in that report.

Mr. Wright replied that there was no truth whatever in it; the company did not contemplate any such action. There had been a meeting of the directors of the company since the disturbance, and they came to the unanimous conclusion that, in the face of the violence offered, it would not be right for them longer to hold their own, as owners of the property, but would be forced into bringing an action against the trespassers.

The Chairman - Then as the representative of the company, you can assure the court that no further obstruction will be placed there till the legal rights of both sides can be ascertained? Mr. Wright – Most certainly.

The Chairman replied that the bench were of opinion that direct excess of force had been used, and that the magistrates had jurisdiction. If it had not been for what had just fallen from the lips of the legal representative of the company they would have felt it their duty to send the case to the sessions for trial, where most likely a severe sentence would have been passed. As it was, the bench could not countenance anything in the shape of a riot. On the occasion in question, the magistrates thought, the police, under Inspector Hindley, had acted in a most admirable manner, and had done exactly that which the law required them to do. The inspector did not lose his presence of mind, but called to many of the people by name, and by that means put a stop to that which most likely would have ended in bloodshed. The bench were further of opinion that he did not use any excess of force, and that in putting handcuffs on the unfortunate person who was manager of the company (Charles Loder) he did what was perfectly right, because in the sight of 2000 or 3000 people he showed the supremacy of the law, and that it must be obeyed. The bench were exceedingly sorry for the three men brought before them, in one sense, but they could not reprobate too strongly their conduct from another point of view. They were acting as the agents of the company, the chairman of which was a member of the local board of health, and were advised by a legal man who was, unhappily, a member of the local board, and who was very recently chairman of that board; all of which circumstances aggravated the case. Those men were employed by the company to commit an excess of violence in what they considered to be an assertion of their rights. The court had, however, nothing to do with the rights on one side or the other, but simply to uphold the peace, which must be preserved. In regards to the defendant Fishwick, it was quite clear that he did not throw stones or brickbats, though he had one in his hand, which he dropped, happily for himself, on seeing the police. The defendants Loder and Fishwick would be bound over to keep the peace for six months – themselves in £100 each, and two sureties in £50 each. Patrick Boyd would be bound over in the same amount, and would, in addition, have to pay a fine of 20s and costs for his assault upon the police officer. In conclusion, Mr. Chambres expressed the hope of the bench that a case of that kind would never again occur in the parish.22

---

22 Liverpool Mercury, 13th December 1877

Transport

Birth of the Ferry

In 1768, as a result of public protest, Liverpool Town Council discontinued the practice of allowing loaded gunpowder wagons to pass through the city streets en route from the port to the Powder House on Brownlow Road (near where Clarence Street is today). They purchased a plot of land near to the safe anchorage lying between Mother Redcap's Inn and Rock Point and built the Liscard Magazines. Every vessel entering the river had to off-load her powder for storage in the magazines until departure and during the unloading; some of the crew would be rowed across to Liverpool. As shipping used the port increased so the patronage of the Magazines grew and by 1820 a thriving passage had developed, much of it unconnected with the storage of gunpowder.

Pleasure seeking Liverpudlians came to sample the unspoilt beaches and a hotel was built together with a number of exclusive residences. The hotel eventually became a school numbering among its fee-paying pupils Menotti and Riciotti Garibaldi, the sons of the Italian patriot. Anyone wanting to conduct business in the vicinity would agree to meet at the ferry. *Gore's Directory* for 1822 advertised a regular service of sailing packets and in 1826 a newly opened Liverpool-Hoylake service, worked by the paddle steamers 'Hero' and 'Paul Pry', called at the Magazines en route.

This service survived until 1832. The absence of a pier at the Magazines ensured that as the other ferries at Egremont and New Brighton were established, the regular service ceased though there were intermittent sailings until the magazine closed in 1851. The gunpowder was transported up river to floating hulks anchored in the Mersey between New Ferry and Eastham. All traces of the stone slipway disappeared during the construction of the new promenade between Holland Road and New Brighton in the 1890s.

New Brighton ferry owed its origins to a Liverpool businessman James Atherton, a retired Everton builder and his son-in-law, William Rowson, a Prescot Solicitor, who advocated the establishment of a ferry service from Liverpool as part of a plan to encourage prospective residents. Situated at the exposed mouth of the Mersey, New Brighton was hardly an ideal location from which to operate an all-year, all tides ferry for it could suffer from high winds and mountainous seas and at low tide the water receded some 650 foot from the shore. Undeterred, score of prosperous Liverpudlians migrated across the water to build comfortable villas with unrivalled views of the Mersey approaches.

In 1833, part of the foreshore was leased from the Commissioners of Woods and Forest and the first wooden pier, which was completed in March 1834, was a curiously-shaped structure extending some 500 foot from the shore. Built of heavy timbers embedded in the rock and supported by a diagonal brace and cross beams, it was 9 feet wide and 30 feet long at its outer extremity. The first 135 feet of the pier was angled north-west; at the river end there was a further 40 foot long structure running due south at which boats could load at high water.

The Ferry, New Brighton

At extreme low water, passengers were forced to wade to and from the steamers but, in 1835, they were carried in a flat-bottomed landing craft which was hauled up and down by a horse-powered windlass. Access to the pier was through a toll house at the shore end or by two flights of steps leading direct from the beach. No formal lease from the Commissioners of Woods and Forests to work the ferry was obtained until April 1851. This extended for 75 years at a rent of one guinea per annum and a grant of 100 yards on each side of the ferry was made on 4th October 1859 for a further guinea per year.

Despite having only one vessel, Atherton advertised an hourly service using a second-hand Scottish-built paddle steamer. 'Sir John Moore'. The journey time for the 2.75 mile crossing was 25 minutes which left little time for turnaround or inclement weather. To provide additional revenue and to supplement the summer schedule, other vessels were permitted to disembark passengers at the pier on payment of a small toll. This practice continued for some 70 years.

In 1838, ownership was transferred to Atherton's two sons who placed the Tranmere-built paddle steamer 'Elizabeth' on the station in 1840. In 1845, they disposed of their interest for £2,000 to the Liverpool firm of Lodge, Pritchard and Co. of which two of the directors were the Coulborn brothers.

Atherton's vision of New Brighton as a suburban Utopia failed to materialise though a few of his fine houses still survive today. Although the ferry had been intended as a residents' link with their workplaces, the facilities tempted droves of working class people to cross at weekends to enjoy a relatively inexpensive day by the sea. Recognising that New Brighton catered for two different types of clientele, the Coulborn's purchased a former gentlemen's yacht 'Queen of Beauty' to provide a superior residents' only service in summer as well as offering elegance and luxury during the winter. She was followed in 1846 by the Liverpool-built 'James Atherton', which, with a capacity of 529, catered for the fluctuations in loading in the summer. Over the next 5 years, the Coulborn's spent over £3,000 on improved facilities. Various extensions to the pier brought passengers to within 80 feet of the low water mark and the old flat bottomed boats were replaced were replaced by a crude version of the running-out stage which comprised a wooden platform running on rails attached by spikes. This clumsy contraption could be raised and lowered over a distance of 200 feet. Sometime in 1848 part of the shore end was damaged by a gale. During the rebuilding, a shack selling anything from tea to wine was erected near the toll house and rented out at £35 per year. Local residents were outraged by this open invitation to imbibe strong liquor and were increasingly concerned by the unchecked growth of the 'Devil's Nest', a row of huts and stalls hugging the high water mark which sold alcoholic drink.

Special constables were sworn in to control the rowdy elements among the day trippers and for over a century many residents resented their influx, feeling that they lowered the tone of an otherwise select neighbourhood.

Following the acquisition of the Egremont ferry lease by the Coulborn's in May 1848, they established their administrative headquarters at Egremont and suspended the New Brighton sailings from 1st October 1849 to Easter 1850 to the disgust of regular users. New Brighton residents were advised to walk along the shore to Egremont. The combination of the two passages resulted in considerable savings in staff and coal and, in winter, doubled the prospective clientele. The Coulborn's received a new lease of the ferry from the Commissioners for Woods and Forests for 75 years from 1851 at a rental of £21 per annum and a grant of 100 yards on each side of the ferry on payment of 21 shillings per annum on 4th October 1859.

New Brighton Pier

The New Brighton Pier was built in 1867 adjacent to the ferry pier on the north side. It was opened on the 7th September, 1867 and completed on the 9th April, 1868. It was 550 feet long and 70 feet wide. It had a pavilion where the Pierrots, Aldeler and Sutton took their shows from the beach. The entrance was through the turnstiles on the ferry pier and people entered as they came off the ferry boat. In the early days, this was the only entrance the promenade pier ending some yards from the promenade. There were Smoking rooms and Rest rooms on the pier and when alterations were carried out in 1913 a new Pavilion was built.

Liverpool Mercury, Tuesday 11th June, 1867

New Promenade Pier at New Brighton

New Brighton has been long noted as a favourite resort for visitors, who, in the summer months especially, crowd the sands in thousands, and enjoy themselves in a variety of ways. Beautifully situated at the mouth of the Mersey, the locality possess attractions of no ordinary character. The sloping shore, extending beyond the Red Noses, affords excellent facilities for bathing, and from the sandhills and elevated ground at the back magnificent views are obtained of the Cheshire and Lancashire coasts, as well as of the boundless expanse of sea in front. During the last quarter of a century the place had undergone a wonderful change for the better. Of late years a great improvement has been effected in the district by the Wallasey Local Board, and palatial residences and splendid hotels and lodging houses have sprung up in every direction. The former miserable landing place was a serious drawback to the prosperity of New Brighton. The local board were

102

fully alive to the importance of the place, and with commendable spirit they applied to Parliament for powers to borrow money to enable them to erect a new landing stage. This power was obtained, and as a result New Brighton now posses a fine landing stage, connected with the shore by an iron pier about 730 feet in length. With good steamers. combined with punctuality in sailing, it may be expected that this charming watering place of the Mersey will attract yearly an increased number of visitors, as well as add greatly to its permanent residents.23

The visitor to New Brighton will now find that another splendid improvement is in progress. This is a magnificent promenade pier which is in course of construction by the New Brighton Pier Company. It will be a similar structure to those at Margate, Blackpool, Brighton, Deal, and other places, all of which have proved highly successful. This new pier was commenced about six months ago, and already it is nearly half completed. It runs parallel with the ferry pier, on the north side, at a distance of 20 feet, and will be 550 feet long, and from 70 to 130 feet wide. It is a most substantial structures. built of iron columns and girders, the columns being sunk in the rocks. The new pier will be approached from the ferry pier by two entrances, each being 30 feet wide, one entrance being at the river end and the other at the shore end. The approach to the promenade pier will be by a flight of broad handsome steps. At each side of these entrances there will be collectors' boxes for the taking of tolls. Opposite each entrance there will be a fine pavilion, constructed in the octagon form, with a clear space of 25 feet on all sides. Running at the back of the centre of the pier there will be a covered saloon, 130 feet in length, and the main portions of it 28 feet in width, extending to 34 feet in the centre. This magnificent apartment will be fitted with glass

23 Liverpool Mercury, Tuesday 11th June, 1867

folding doors, and form a fine promenade in itself during unfavourable weather. It is also intended to make this saloon available for a variety of purposes, such as refreshment rooms, bazaars, flower shows, concerts, etc. Over the saloon there will be a promenade of the same dimensions, with a magnificent tower built in the Byzantine style of architecture, which will give the whole structure a handsome and striking appearance. At each end of the saloon there will be an elegant glass weather screen, intended for the protection of visitors while sitting in the open air. On the north side, and opposite the large saloon, the pier will widen into the form of a semi-circle or embayment, which will make the structure at this point 130 feet wide. The deck of the pier will be covered with a sort of concrete, to render it comfortable by walking in wet weather; and a line of comfortable seats, of handsome design, will extend round the entire structure, which will be 5 feet above the level of the ferry pier. From the deck of the new pier an uninterrupted view of the sea, the river, the shipping, and the busy and populous town on the other side will be obtained.

The work, as we have already stated, is of a most substantial character. The engineer is Mr. E. Birch, of London, who has successfully completed similar piers at other watering places; and the contractor is Mr. J.E. Dowson, also of London. If deemed desirable, one-half of the pier might be opened to the public in August next but the contractor is bound to complete the whole work by the end of the present year.

The New Brighton Pier Company deserves great credit for the spirit they have exhibited in proceeding with this undertaking in the face of much difficulty. This splendid promenade pier is sure to attract immense numbers of people to New Brighton, by which the ferry will reap a rich harvest. Under these circumstances it seems somewhat strange that but few residents of the locality have taken up shares in the undertaking, the greater portion of the capital being subscribed by Manchester gentlemen, who no doubt have looked upon the matter in a practical point of view, and calculated, from the success of such piers in other places, upon realising a handsome return for their outlay.

New Brighton Pier.

The pier closed in 1923 and four years later the Wallasey Corporation became its new owners and re-opened it with its own entrance from the promenade. The whole of the pier was rebuilt in 1931 at a cost of £45,000.

As in other resorts the pier had its own theatre, it was not built to high standards but some good turns could be seen on its stage. The theatre was about 130 feet in length and was used for Concerts, Flower Shows and the like. Various shows were held there during the 1800's and towards the end of the century. At the end of the 1908 season the theatre was closed down for general improvements on the decor, seats and stage, there was even heating installed!! The theatre reopened on 15th March 1909.

New Brighton Pier

Some early films were shown between acts and a short season of plays were staged, in the winter now the theatre had heating installed pantomimes were performed with great success.

Pier, New Brighton.

As other theatres on the resort attracted larger crowds the Pavilion theatre died off and was eventually closed in 1923. The closure of the New Brighton Ferry affected the life of the promenade pier.

Fortes Limited became the owners in 1968, carrying out repairs and it continued for a time, but it was not a paying proposition.

After much discussion, the pier was dismantled in 1978, the ferry pier having been demolished some five years earlier.

The Ferries & the Railways

The railways regarded New Brighton as a potential source of traffic as the resort grew in popularity but the lack of a branch line limited their options. The Local Board in August 1878 endorsed an agreement with the Cheshire Lines Committee for the issue of through tickets between stations in the Manchester area and New Brighton throughout the year, passengers making their own way between Liverpool Central station and the landing stage.

In July 1879 a similar arrangement was made with the London and North Western Railway for the month of July 1880 only, no further arrangements being made with that company for many years. Some bookings involved two ferry trips, from Woodside to Liverpool then to New Brighton. In 1889, by which time there were amenities at New Brighton, the management were pressing the railways and agreements were made with other companies, including the Liverpool Overhead Railway with who through tickets were offered in both directions as the round trip on the 'Overhead' giving unrivalled views of ships in the docks was a popular pastime with Wallasey people. These were the first through fares to be reinstated in 1922 after wartime suspension. The success of these through bookings depended on their promotion by the railway companies in the inland towns and the Local Board in some cases agreed to contribute towards these costs. The ferries' share of through ticket was usually 4 old pence. Revenue from through railway passengers was given as £1,278.50 which represents 76,710 return journeys but unfortunately it is not clear what period this covered. Through tram ticket from St

Helens, involving two trams each way, were introduced in 1905 and continued until 1939.

From 1st July 1900 special summer only tickets between the three Wallasey ferries and Eastham were offered at 6d, 7d and 8d. In the first month 1,184 were sold but patronage gradually declined and the agreement lapsed in 1913. Through tickets were issued including admission to various attractions at New Brighton such as the Tower Ballroom, the Palace and the Promenade Pier.

Competition for New Brighton ferry

Although there had been plans to build railways to both Seacombe and New Brighton in the 1850s and 1860s, these had lapsed and it was not until 1881 that the Seacombe, Hoylake and Deeside Railway obtained parliamentary powers to construct a line from Bidston to Seacombe, following this is 1882 and 1886 with other schemes for Wallasey and New Brighton. These lines were not a threat to the ferries until three interconnecting lines were brought into use on 2nd January 1888. These were the Mersey Railway's branch from Hamilton Square to Birkenhead Park, the Wirral Railway's Birkenhead Park-Docks line and the Seacombe, Hoylake and Deeside line thence to Wallasey which was extended to a station at Atherton Street, New Brighton on 30th March 1888. Connecting trains with some through carriages brought New Brighton to within 25 minutes of the centre of Liverpool. The original plan to bring the trains down to Rowson Street was never carried out, because of the gradient and shortage of funds, so the station was inconveniently situated for many residents.

The Mersey Railway had deprived Woodside and Tranmere ferries of many thousands of passengers since its opening in February 1886 but, although it was unaffected by the weather and took passengers further into Liverpool, it had certain disadvantages, mainly the sulphurous fumes from the locomotives in the tunnel which gradually worsened over the years despite all kinds of expensive ventilation measures taken by the company. Furthermore, not all trains had through carriages and connections at Birkenhead Park (which was dubbed Pneumonia Junction by sufferers) were not always maintained. After the Wirral and the Mersey Railways fell out for a time in the 1890s, the through carriages ceased altogether.

The ferries had been experiencing a slump in revenue before the railway had opened. The takings in 1885-1886 being £2,000 below the previous year's. In both 1887-1888 and 1888-1889 revenue at about £44,000 was £5,000 down on 1884-1885. New Brighton, which was dependant on good weather, fell from £27,000 in 1886-1887 to £20,500 in 1889-1889, 24% down, much of it due to railway competition. Wallasey ferries implemented various economy measures which included a reduction in manning levels in June 1886 and halving of the bonuses paid to masters and engineers. Holidays were reduced from two weeks to one week and the manager's salary was cut from £425 to £350 per annum.

'Express' boats were introduced to run direct to and from New Brighton in anticipation of the competition from the railway. The boats ran from February 1887 between 7.15 and 9.50am and 5.00 and 7.00pm. In January 1888 a monthly contract was offered at 7s 6d (37½p) and other fare concessions were made. However, the cost of these measures exceeded the benefits and the direct boats had all been withdrawn by August 1888. From 1st October to 1893 to 28th February 1894 the experiment was repeated with no more success and again from 1st May 1899 when a half-hourly all-day direct service was started and lasted until the end of summer 1900. The experiment was never revived. Over 1.5 million passengers deserted the ferries for the trains and it was 11 years before the revenue fully recovered. However, the worst of the financial crisis had been overcome by February 1890 when holiday, salary and bonus cuts were restored in full. Some passengers came back from the railway to the ferry but they had a difficult choice. In the winter they could either freeze at 'Pneumonia Junction' and suffocate in the tunnel or face the full fury of the river at its most malignant.

New Brighton Terminal Problems

The growth of seasonal traffic at New Brighton by 1879 swamped the facilities and at Whitsuntide the crush was so great that some boats had to be sent back to Liverpool without unloading the passengers. Four boats were hired on this occasion as well as 2 tugs, the Woodside streamer 'Liverpool' and a Tranmere vessel for beaching as a stage extension at Egremont. The Board accepted plans by the well known engineer, Dowson, in October 1879 for a new stage measuring 240ft by 55ft and a second passenger bridge for £6,500. But there was a backwash from ratepayers and the Board were obliged to cease with the plans for the time being, instead spending a small amount on repairs to maintain the existing conditions.

The Local Board in 1881 succeeded in raising a loan of £8,500 and Dowson prepared a modified scheme for a stage 220ft long but it was February 1884 before the contract for the work was awarded to Head, Wrightson & co. for £7,327. This embraced an additional bridge, enlarged landing stage, strengthening and alterations to the main pier and a pay gate access. To take the strain of the new bridge the pier was strengthened which was placed at an angle of 15 degrees to the north-east of the existing bridge and attached to the enlarged floating stage by well-lubricated sliding plates. There were four balanced gangways and two vessels could load or unload simultaneously. These improvements and the increase in the number of reversible turnstiles greatly reduced overcrowding.

The Board wanted the work finished by Good Friday 1885 and accused Dowson of spending too little time on the project. The deadline was not met, the two bridges being put in position on 23rd April and the whole job was not completed until 30th July. The estimate was exceeded by £3,440 though this included £1,196 for new shelters on the stage and turnstiles which were not in the original budget. But all was not well. Soon after the official reopening, the stage was strengthened to avoid serious damage by heavier steamers and by 1888 was said to be in poor condition. By 1896, a report by consulting engineer J.J Webster revealed serious weakness in the whole structure which was in urgent need of major repairs.

In 1900 Allsup's of Preston were awarded a £6,000 contract to replace the northern bridge, which was originally built in 1866, and to widen the pier alongside the toll booths so that more of them could be provided. The work was done during the winter, the new steel passenger bridge being lifted into position on 27th December 1900. A new southern bridge, built by Heenan and Froude of Manchester was installed on 29th August 1907 and the northern bridge and the stage twice needed repairs following the March gales of 1907 and others in November 1908.

The New Brighton service was plagued during the 1890s by insufficient depth of water at low tide and much time was spent in trying to find a solution. Contacts with the Dock Board brought forth no assistance. In March 1895 the manager tried to hire a dredger from the Ribble Navigation but this fell through. Formal permission to dredge the river was given by the Mersey Conservancy Board and enquiries about dredging were made as far afield as Irvine and Whitby. An offer by the Manchester Ship Canal Co. for the hire of a dredger for £1,000 per month was considered too expensive. The manager calculated revenue losses caused by suspension of the service and, on the strength of this; in June 1896 it was decided to seek a loan of £10,000 to purchase a suction dredger. An order was eventually placed with T. Walker of Sudbrook, Mon. and the vessel, named 'Tulip', having been launched on 28th September 1897, was delayed by a strike and problems with her equipment, which included a Gwynne's Pump. She was a substantial vessel of 432 gross tons measuring 160ft long by 27ft 1in and she started work at New Brighton on 12th May 1898. Initially there were doubts about her ability to tackle the marl and clay deposits at Egremont, another dredger, 'Sicily' being hired. A dispute with her builders finally went to arbitration. As much as 23,000 cubic yards, of sand was removed by dredging in February 1901, resulting in 40 passenger crossings being cancelled. A further 29,000 cubic yards were removed in August 1904.

A plan to lengthen the pier was turned down by the Conservator who advised the Council to 'pursue a policy of much more active dredging'. However, at Easter 1905, the traffic was so heavy, revenue being 22.5% higher than the previous year; doubtless the weather played a part. Unfortunately on the Monday, an exceptionally low tide resulted in the suspension of the ferry service at New Brighton for much of the afternoon and evening, resulting in Seacombe having a record day, 106,119 adult fare-paying passengers through the turnstiles. The tram services between Seacombe and New Brighton were filled to capacity. In November 1906 the Council decided to borrow £10,000 to fiancé dredging and employed a consulting engineer, A.F. Fowler, who recommended scraping the river bed with a bucket dredger. In February 1907 a contract was given to the Tilbury Contracting and Dredging Co. to keep the approaches clear throughout the year. The bucket dredger 'Beaufort' lifted 45,000 cubic yards of hard material including mussel shale in the early months of 1907. While the work was in progress, a violent storm on 16th March tore the stage from its mooring and drove it out to sea. The south end bridge and several pontoons were badly damaged. The stage was salvaged the following day and towed into dry dock for repair.

Temporary landing arrangements obliged the ferry to close two hours before each low tide, seriously affecting traffic on Good Friday and Easter Saturday. However, more or less normal services were restored on the Monday and thousands of pleasure seekers were carried from Liverpool, the two luggage boats being pressed into service in addition to the ordinary passenger steamers.

By 10th June 1907 dredging operations were completed and, by the end of May, 42,784 cubic yards. of material had been removed

115

giving an average depth of 11-12ft. 'Tulip' had assisted 'Beaufort' for which the contractors reimbursed the ferries, and, in January 1908, she was fitted with a new section pump so that she could maintain the new depth of water. In 1911-1912 sand eroders were placed underwater by which time boats could approach at almost all states of the stage. She was very successful in keeping New Brighton and Egremont landing stages free of silt and on occasions she was hired to Birkenhead Corporation who had similar difficulties at Rock Ferry. She was hired to Wexford Harbour Board in 1903 for £400 per month, being insured for £10,000 for the voyage. Later in the year she worked at Heysham and in 1906 at Port Talbot. 'Tulip' removed 63,000 cubic yards. of sand and shale in 1911 and the effectiveness of her value to the undertaking was demonstrated when she had to cease work during the coal strike of 1912 and 'Snowdrop' had to be grounded alongside the stage.

Wallasey Tramways

A New Route to New Brighton

Wallasey Urban District Council had decided in 1896 to introduce municipally-operated electric tramways and had instructed their District Engineer and Surveyor, W. H Travers, to draw up plans. He recommended a system that would provide three different routes linking Seacombe Ferry to New Brighton (via Seabank Road, via Rake Lane, and via Seaview Road and Warren Drive). These were approved by the Council's newly-formed Tramways Committee at its first meeting on 12 May 1898, and application was subsequently made to Parliament. They were authorised in the Wallasey Tramways and Improvements Act 1899, but owing to stiff resistance from the United Company the Council did not take over the horse tramways until midnight on 30 March 1901.

The 1899 Act authorised 8.5 miles of standard gauge tramways. Corresponding exactly with the initial system opened in 1902. The double track sections (mainly passing loops) totalled just under two miles, the rest being single track (mainly used in both directions) but with one-way working in separate streets approaching the two terminus. Most of the passing places were of two-car length (88 yards). The depot was to be built on land off Seaview Road adjacent to the Council's electricity generating station, with separate two-storey administrative offices fronting on to Seaview Road. The estimated cost was £72,821 including track at £2,189 per mile, paving at £2,229 per mile, £9,000 for cars and £5,129 for the depot.

The Tramways Committee, having appointed sub-committees to deal with specific issues, decided to adopt standard gauge (4ft 8½in) and overhead current collection. Visits were made to inspect tramways at Glasgow, Leeds, Liverpool, Halifax and Hull and to the Preston works of the Electric Railway and Tramway Carriage Works Ltd. (ER&TCW). The initial requirements were 20 trams and the Committee considered the following tenders:

Electric Railway & Tramway Carriage Works Ltd.
£11,800 without air brakes or £12,700 with air brakes
British Westinghouse Electric & Manufacturing Co.
£11,940 plus £1,000 for air brakes
Brush Electrical Engineering Company
£13,200 without air brakes
Robert W. Blackwell & Co. Ltd.
£13,925 with air brakes

The committee accepted the first tender, without air brakes, as the Board of Trade had meanwhile ruled that despite grades of 1 in 15 and 1 in 16 the cars would need neither air nor slipper brakes.

During the legal battle with the Company, work had begun on the future Seabank Road line. The first rail of the new system was laid in King Street on 24 June 1901 by W. G. Ellery, new Chairman of the Council. The track bed was excavated, and buildings demolished at the corner of Seabank Road and Trafalgar Road to accommodate an S-shaped length of double track. The Council used direct labour, and the men completed a mile of single track per month.

On 20 February 1901, Major (later Lt.Col) Robert Roughley Greene, aged 48, was appointed Tramway Manager, at a salary of £250 per year. He had been accountant with the Dock Board, and was general secretary of the Liverpool Dispensaries. He came from a local family and, having been chairman of the UDC in 1897, was fully conversant with municipal procedure. He also commanded the New Brighton Company of the 1st Cheshire and Caernarvonshire Artillery volunteers, a predecessor of the Territorial Army.

As owners of the tracks used by the horse trams, the Council had already re-laid much of the horse car route between 1897 and 1898 with heavier rail suitable for electric cars, but all passing loops, junctions, and sections not scheduled for electrification had been left untouched, with the result that repairs had to be carried out in May 1901. Meanwhile, new tracks were laid to form the anti-clockwise "horse-shoe" or "Balloon" loops outside New Brighton ferry, as well as the connecting length between Molyneux Drive and the horse tram terminus at Field Road which was completed by late September 1901. Work began on 16 August on the line between St. Paul's Church, Seacombe and the Falkland Road/Liscard Road corner which took two months and involved a new street, Mainwaring Road, directly linking Lloyd's Corner and Liscard Road.

The Falkland Road horse car line was closed from 9 September 1901 and trams used Church Street in both directions; this allowed new track to be laid in the very narrow part of Liscard Road between Falkland Road and Church Street. The successive diversions of the horse cars between this point and Seacombe Ferry in the last weeks of 1901 included a horse car service along the electric tracks from Seacombe to Molyneux Drive via Seabank Road which commenced on 1 December 1901, permitting work to begin on the renewal of loops and point work along part of the original horse tramway between Church Street and Field Road, with major road widening in Liscard Village and Rake Lane. When this work was complete, the horse trams reverted to their original route and the construction teams joined those already at work on the Seaview Road portion of the Warren Drive route.

Except for the track laid by R. W. Blackwell & Co Ltd in the car sheds and along the depot approach road, all other track-laying was under the supervision of Council engineer W. H. Travers and his two assistants, Howdle and Jackson. Laid on a concrete bed 6in thick, the rails 7 in deep with a 1⅛ in groove weighed 98lb/yd and were supplied in 60ft lengths by Barrow Haematite Steel Co Ltd, costing £7 7s. 6d per ton, with 37lb soleplates and 24-inch six-hole fishplates. Askham Bros. and Wilson Ltd. supplied the points and crossings, tie-bars, fish bolts, drain boxes and Dawson's patent drain rail, the points being 8ft 6in long and the crossings being of crucible cast steel. Special work was pre-assembled to specification on a concrete platform in the Council's yard in Mill

Lane. Anchors were placed under rails on the steeper gradients, the most severe being the 1 in 15 out of New Brighton terminus and for a 20 yard stretch of Rowson Street. Transition curves were employed; the sharpest had a radius of 40ft in the centre of the curve. Brown's rail bonds were used and flexible "Crown" cross bonds were installed at all points and crossings and at 100ft intervals on plain track. The paving used was 4in to 6in granite setts, except for Allcott's 5in hardwood blocks on the most select stretch of Seabank Road.

The feeder cables (11 miles) supplied by the British Insulated Wire Co. Ltd. were laid and joined by the Council's staff, in single earthenware troughs filled with bitumen. The overhead equipment was supplied and installed by R. W. Blackwell & Co. Ltd., using 400 poles bought from the British Mannesmann company. the standard poles tapered in three sections from 7in to 5¼in outside diameter, but heavy poles of 8in to 6in diameter were used for pull-offs at curves; the bases were of cast iron with a neat scroll and the Tramways monogram (WCT) artistically entwined. Span wire construction, side poles with bracket arms elsewhere; the bracket arms varied in length from 10ft 6in to 18ft 6in included ornamental scrollwork and rosettes to take arc lamps if required. The trolley wire of 3/0 gauge hard drawn copper was hung 21ft above road level. The overhead included guard wires of 7/16in galvanised steel, bonded to the poles and rails at every fifth pole. Telephone wires linking the depot with Seacombe and New Brighton were carried on insulators fixed to the bracket arms. Cast iron rectangular section boxes bearing the Council monogram contained switches and fuses for the feeders and the overhead lines.

The first of the 20 new electric cars were delivered complete at Wallasey Station in mid-January 1902, and were dragged along Grove Road and Hose Side Road by teams of horses; the wheels gouging grooves in the surface. All subsequent deliveries were to Liscard & Poulton station. At the end of February it was announced that the Seabank Road and Rake Lane routes would open in mid-March, with Warren Drive to follow later on. On Saturday 8 March a tour of inspection was held for Council Officials and representatives of the construction firms. Driver training was now in progress, some men having previous experience at Birkenhead or Liverpool, others being Irish labourers formerly employed in the track laying gangs.

The Board of trade inspection took place on Friday 14 March 1902, the inspectors being Major Druitt RE for cars and track and Mr. A. P. Trotter for the electrical installations. The party assembled at the depot at 9.45am, and the inspectors accompanied by Greene, Travers, Council officials and representatives of the contractors boarded car No 10 and departed first to Seacombe via

125

Wheatland Lane. The car then proceeded to New Brighton via Rake Lane and back to Seacombe via Seabank Road. The inspection was completed by taking the car along Liscard Road to the top of Church Street, reversing and returning to Seacombe via Brighton Street. Having witnessed an emergency stop and examined all track and overhead junctions, especially those at either end of Rowson Street hill, the inspectors declared themselves satisfied, except for the "horseshoe" at New Brighton where the curve on the south side was too sharp. Temporary terminal arrangements were still in force there in late April.

The System Opens

With the inspection successfully concluded, Wallasey Council officials announced that public service would begin on the Rake Lane route at 8am on Monday 17 March. The intervening weekend was spent completing driver training and running cars at frequent intervals along both routes. There was an increasing sense of excitement in the town as people prepared to welcome the new electric cars.

Leaving Seaview Road depot at 7.30am on Monday morning to take up duty at the 8am from New Brighton, the first car lost its trolley head whilst reversing at Liscard. A second car was hastily despatched and left New Brighton at 8.10am. Between 8.30am and 9am another car derailed, finishing on the footpath near Osborne Avenue, whilst in a third mishap a car jumped the points at the foot of Rowson Street, narrowly missing the frontage of the North and South Wales Bank on the opposite corner. There were no injuries, and a ten minute service was provided until 11.45pm.

The opening ceremony, attended by dignitaries from all over Merseyside, was held two days later on 19 March when the Seabank Road route was inaugurated. At noon, the Chairman of the Tramway Committee, Dr. T. W. A Napier and other council members, officials and guests assembled at Seacombe Ferry and after declaring the system open from the top deck of a decorated car, travelled past lines of schoolchildren to New Brighton via Seabank Road, returning along Rake Lane to Liscard Village and the depot. Dr. Napier drove the car, and apparently the circuit breaker blew whilst ascending Rowson Street. The car started to run back, and he quickly brought it to a standstill by applying the emergency short-circuits brake.

After inspecting the depot and power plant the party then made their way to the Council offices in Church Street for lunch. After the loyal toast, Mr Ellery, Chairman of the Council, proposed "The Wallasey Tramways." In his speech he said that the system must not be considered complete until a line had been built to serve Wallasey Village. Replying, Dr. Napier confessed that elation was tinged with anxiety until the tramway had proved itself. He professed total confidence in the quality of workmanship and defended the Council's policy of supporting English firms even if they were a little more expensive than their foreign competitors. As for Wallasey Village, he assured Mr. Ellery that this would be attended to as soon as possible. Public service started immediately between Seacombe and New Brighton via Seabank Road, and the press were fulsome in their praise - "a few mishaps, but they must inevitably be anticipated when first enslaving and domesticating such a fickle power of electricity."

In their first week of operation the trams carried 60,000 people, and in the first full month nearly 400,000, almost equally divided between the two routes. The single track and loops soon proved to be inadequate. As in Birkenhead, demand had been underestimated, and Wallasey had the additional problem of seasonal holiday traffic. As early as Easter 1902 the 17 available trams had failed to shift the crowds, and the third route - Warren Drive - was not yet in operation. It was inspected and opened on 17

May 1902, completing the initial programme, and was the third line to connect Seacombe with New Brighton.

The Manager recommended the purchase of five bogie single deck combination cars, for which Dick Kerr had quoted £585; however, the Tramways Committee overruled him and an order was placed for five more double-deckers identical to No 1 - 20, plus a multi-purpose works car. These became 21-25 and the works car 26.

Large crowds were carried during the 1902 holiday season - 125,000 in Whit Week and 140,000 in early August, but these were exceeded by the 160,000 carried during the Coronation week of Edward VII. From September there was a seasonal downturn, with only 85,000 travelling during the week beginning 13 December. The electrification had stimulated social and economic change; building development increased, leading to a boom in land and property prices, the most sought after residences being those within easy reach of a tram stop. More people chose to live in Wallasey and work in Liverpool. Equally, many now found it cheaper to shop in Liverpool, which led to the slow decline of some of the older commercial thoroughfares such as Borough Road, Brighton Street and King Street.

Most of the traffic was towards the three ferries, with Seacombe capturing the lion's share. Patronage on the Egremont and New Brighton boats declined, to the charging of the Ferries Committee, who saw the trams as a potential threat to the future of the two northern stations. Both ferries were reached by long. Exposed piers on which passengers could be soaked or buffeted by ferocious winds and although Egremont had its quota of regular commuters, it was not surprising that all but the hardiest opted for a tram journey to Seacombe with its short all-weather crossing.

In November 1902 it was agreed that the trams should carry flags tied to their trolley ropes to warn passengers when the northern boats had been suspended due to "stress of weather". One wit claimed that the Tramways Committee had only agreed so that they could demonstrate the superior service offered by their trams. A square blue flag meant "No boat from New Brighton" and a red swallow-tail "No boat from Egremont." Red metal discs were hoisted on various traction poles for the same purpose, at the top of Tobin Street, the top of Church Street, Grove Road/Warren Drive corner and at several points along Victoria Road. The Tramways Committee refused to allow ferry contract holders to travel free when the boats were suspended.

Relations between the Ferries and Tramways Committees in Wallasey were in sharp contrast to Birkenhead, where direct competition from the Mersey Railway had forced them to co-operate for their mutual protection. In Wallasey, no combined bus/ferry fares were introduced until 1928. However, both committees accepted that the public expected regular and reliable service, and from 12 July 1902 timetables were adjusted to guarantee connections at Seacombe between the ten-minute boats and the ten-minute trams. This was to remain a guiding principle throughout the life of the tramways; everything was geared to meeting the boats on time. Late running was penalised and delays thoroughly investigated.

Stretches of single line, especially when shared by two services, worked against this and Greene lost no opportunity to argue the case for double track wherever possible. He presented several reports on the subject, advocating the use of parallel or neighbouring streets for one-way working was already adopted at both Seacombe and New Brighton. Plans for doubling virtually the entire network were prepared for inclusion in a new Tramways and Improvement Act to be presented to Parliament in 1904, but the Bill provoked such opposition from residents and householders that it proved impossible to acquire frontages for road widening, and was abandoned. Despite this, major track doubling was carried out during 1903-04 without specific Parliamentary sanction, increasing the total of double track to 3.38 miles by March 1905, and is best described by taking each route in turn.

At the shortest route linking New Brighton and Seacombe, this always carried the heaviest traffic, serving all three ferry stations and the area of greatest residential density and commercial development. Originally the journey time had been 20 minutes, but in the summer months it was extended to 23 minutes. The ten minute headway was found to be inadequate, especially in peak hours, and a five minute evening service was introduced on 12 July 1902 between Molyneux Drive and Seacombe and was later extended to the morning peak, with a 7½ minute frequency between 10am and 1.30pm. Additional passing loops were put in at Rice Lane and Hale Road in the summer of 1902, and by 1904 the lines were doubled from Brougham Road to Falkland Road and from Rice Lane to Maddock Road. Some of the bracket poles were replaced by span wiring. A loop was laid at the top of Tobin Street, with an outbound-only connection into Church Street, and a crossover was installed at Trafalgar Road for part-way working. Other loops were added at Lincoln Drive (1904) and Magazine Lane (1907). At the same time, the main feeder from Manor Road to Holland Road was renewed. Greene also wanted to double the track in the narrowest part of King Street, but it proved impossible to acquire sufficient frontages.

This line picked up a certain amount of holiday overflow traffic from New Brighton but its main source was from the increasingly important shopping centre at Liscard together with passengers from Central Park and the Cemetery. Operationally the most difficult section was the length of Liscard Road from St. John's Church to Liscard Village which it shared with the Warren Drive cars, as there were blind corners at either end of the only one passing loop, at Martin's Lane. As early as September 1902, Greene advocated building a relief line for outbound Rake Lane cars along Manor Road and Grosvenor Street, but it was not adopted. During the winter of 1903-04 the double track on Liscard Road was extended to run from Littledale Road to Lathom Avenue which gave outbound drivers approaching Liscard a clear view of the narrow part of Liscard Road. A short length of interlaced track, the first in Wallasey, was laid between Church Street and Falkland Road being replaced by double lines when the gardens of houses were acquired in 1907. A single point allowed outbound Warren Drive cars to turn out from Church Street. Wooden blocks were laid outside the Central Hospital to reduce noise, and side brackets were replaced by span wires. Throughout its life, the Rake Lane route ran every ten minutes, and required six cars, supplemented at rush hours by three extras. The journey time was 26 minutes.

When first introduced, the Warren Drive cars operated only every fifteen minutes, with four cars and a journey time of 28 minutes, Loadings initially were light, producing 6.72d per car mile compared with 8.71d on Rake Lane and 10d on Seabank Road, reflecting the fact that Warren Drive cars operated through an area of low-density high class residential property. However, Greene accurately predicted an increase in the summer when the line would offer unspoilt views of the whole Mersey Estuary and the Welsh hills. North of Liscard there were two loops on the way to the depot, and six more before the rote rejoined the others at New Brighton. The three loops along Warren Drive itself at Ennerdale Road, Stonebark and near Atherton Street were all "blind", and a fourth loops was added at North Drive (Warren Point) in 1903. The service frequency was improved to ten minutes in May 1905.

Warren Drive cars left Seacombe via Demesne Street, sharing the track with the Seabank Road cars as far as Egremont and then traversing Church Street to reach Liscard Road. The two way single track along Church Street with its blind corners at either end proved a serious miscalculation. It was especially hazardous in fog, delays building up at the busy Tobin Street junction, Congestion also occurred every time a boat landed at Egremont, with people walking up the hill to wait for a tram. By December 1902, inbound Warren Drive cars were diverted to operate via Lloyd's Corner, leading to complaints from shopkeepers along Brighton Street. In 1904, as part of a plan to restore trams to Falkland Road (used by horse cars until September 1901) and to encourage greater use of Egremont ferry, it was proposed to lay two sidings in Tobin Street, with connecting tracks into Church Street, King Street and Church Road. The scheme was rejected, but demands continued to be made for a bus or tram route to serve Egremont ferry approach.

In May 1905 the last few yards of single track in Brighton Street (from Church Street to Falkland Road) were doubled, and in July the Council approved the construction of a single track line along Falkland Road, at a cost of £2,050. They rejected an alternative scheme to widen Church Street. The 0.25 mile line was authorised in the Wallasey Tramways and Improvement Act 1906 and work began on 3 January 1907. The line was inspected and opened for use by Seacombe bound Warren Drive cars on 2 May 1907. The fourth tram route, to Poulton and Wallasey Village, did not materialise until 1910-11.

Greene's first Annual Report was presented in March 1903, and established several financial precedents. With an operating surplus of £12,000, the Council wisely agreed to the creation of a Sinking Fund and a Depreciation and Renewal Fund, into which a percentage of the profit was deposited annually. In the following year a sum was also transferred for relief of the rates. The life-blood of the system was the 1d penny, which encouraged ridership on a large scale. 70% of all tickets sold were 1d, 29.02% 2d and 0.08% 2d workmen's returns, with total receipts of £31,475.

Expenditure amounted to £19,194 made up of wages £13,951, energy £6,630, maintenance £1,150, works staff wages £1,276, and track repairs £76.The cars had run 654,742 miles, carried 5,685,182 passengers at an average fare of 1.3 pence. The construction costs to date including track, overhead, cars and buildings were £120,503 of which £109,000 had been raised by loans, repayments in the first year being £3,773.

On 5 April 1907 certain penny stages were extended; Seacombe to Manor Road (in lieu of Trafalgar Road), Falkland Road, and Egremont to Hose Side (in lieu of St. John's Church to Hose Side). In the following year 250,000 more penny tickets were sold on this route, but this was offset by a drop of 130,000 in 2d sales, a loss of £64. To handle the additional traffic extra mileage had cost £394, an overall loss of £458. Councillors frequently failed to acknowledge the financial consequences of their vote-catching exercises. In April 1908 the Council sanctioned a penny stage from Egremont to New Brighton (in lieu of Molyneux Drive) but postponed a decision on extending the Manor Road 1d stage to Holland Road when the Tramways Committee warned of a considerable "shrinking in revenue".

Between 1903 and 1908 the fleet was augmented by the delivery of a further 14 cars. To carry the growing traffic, especially at peak hours, Wallasey expanded its use of part-way cars which, by 1905-06, accounted for a 5.2% increase in overall mileage. Each route had a number of intermediate termini, some more regularly used that others, Seabank Road usually had a 'part-way' following the through car as far as Molyneux Drive, another to Holland Road and occasionally a third to Trafalgar Road. Rake Lane had no advertised 'part-ways' but cars were occasionally turned at Liscard Village, (known as Wallasey Road), at Earlston Road and at Mount Pleasant Road (Stroud's Corner); on Saturdays there were regular inbound part-way cars to Lloyd's Corner. Warren Drive had 'part-ways' to Grasmere Drive (the depot), Earlston Road, Hose Side (or 'Hoe Side') and Grove Road/Warren Drive junction. All these destinations other than Lloyd's Corner were followed by the suffix "Only." Originally wooden or brass part-way plates were hung on the bulkhead guard-rails but these were eventually replaced by small boards showing the part-way terminus attached to the rear dash by tiny brass chains.

Despite these arrangements, the manager was asked to refute an allegation made to the Board of Trade that cars were being overcrowded. He conceded that some overcrowding was inevitable at rush hours, in the high season and in wet weather, but maintained it was impossible to provide every passenger with a seat since many, despite the ample provision of part-ways, chose to travel on the leading car, leaving the duplicate half empty. Wallasey trams carried 9.17 passengers per car mile, about the average for the whole country.

Unlike Birkenhead, Wallasey trams carried few industrial workers. Most of the passengers were white-collar employees travelling to and from Liverpool, with peaks between 8am and 9am and (the heaviest) between 5pm and 6pm. There was a third peak between 10pm and 11pm with people returning home from places of entertainment. However, from 24 March 1902, a half-hourly service for 'Artisans, mechanics or daily labourers' was operated to Seacombe from Molyneux Drive and Liscard Village (Wallasey Road), starting at 5.12am. Initially only a 2d workmen's return was sold on any car departing before 8am, but a 1d single ticket was introduced later. This enabled the unemployed who crossed to Liverpool in search of work but were unsuccessful to return home before the 2d ticket became valid at 4pm. From 13 May 1907 the Seabank Road departure were extended to Victoria Road/Rowson Street, operating every 15 minutes from 5.05am. Following a short-lived extension to Rake Lane (at Earlston Road) the other early morning cars re-scheduled to start at the depot. They were supplemented by March 1908 (and probably from 18 December 1907) by a half-hourly service from Grove Road/Warren Drive, starting at 7.03am. Later, with the opening of the Poulton route cars were left the same point travelling via Wallasey Village from 4.42am (later 4.56am). This pattern continued 'virtually unchanged to abandonment. Although providing a necessary service, only an average of 1,100 per day used the early cars and of these 60% purchased the 1d single ticket.

The tramways augmented their ordinary revenue by hiring cars for use by private parties. The first known hire was on 15 October 1902 when the Committee agreed to convoy 600 children free of charge from Seacombe to Clifton Hall on the occasion of a visit by Lord Strathcona of the Navy League. With the opening in 1911 of the tramway to Harrison Drive demand for hire cars increased and by the year ending 31 March 1912 7,660 passengers had been carried over 687 car miles for £64 at a rate of 22.36d per mile. The usual large load required five or six cars; however a Liverpool Sunday School outing required 12 cars to convey 793 children. From 1 April 1912 hire charges were revised to 10s per car for a return trip over a 1d stage and 15s over a 2d stage. There was a reduction for cars carrying 60 0r over. The rates were again revised in July 1913 to 10s 6d per 1d stage, 15s 6d for a 2d stage and 21s for the new 3d stage.

The year 1907 saw major improvements to both the principal termini. As the loop at Seacombe was meant to handle three services it is surprising that it was designed with no sidings or loops; trams arrived at the ferry via Church Road, traversed the loop in a clockwise direction and left via Demesne Street (the reverse of the flow envisaged in the 1988 Act). Cars therefore had to depart in the order they arrived, and any breakdown there would cause major delays.

A siding, first used on 18 June 1902, was soon added on the south side of Victoria Place to enable the more frequent Seabank Road cars to overtake others, and in February/March 1907 the tracks on the north side were re-aligned to include a passing loop and a short dead-end stub for disabled cars. Inspectors could now regulate car movements before despatching them to the departure tracks. A facing crossover was laid at the foot of Church Road for emergency use, and a curve was built later linking Demesne Street to the north side of the loop, probably to provide for a suggested reversal of the flow into Seacombe urged in July 1911 by the Brighton Street traders. A six-month experiment was envisaged, but there is no evidence that it took place. No further alterations were necessary at Seacombe, despite the peak-hour provision from 1911 of some eleven cars to meet each 10-minute boat.

At New Brighton, the Tramways Department was faced by two problems; firstly the terminal loop and secondly the one-way system in and out of the resort. The anti-clockwise 'Horse Shoe' (a name first given to the pier approaches in 1864) was inconvenient and inflexible, as cars were again obliged to leave in the order they arrived, and there was nowhere to park spare trams. From 29 March 1907 the loop was replaced by the grid-iron of four sidings each capable of accommodating two cars. A curve was also added from Virginia Road to Victoria Road allowing some cars to by-pass the grid-iron, especially on bank holidays. Two of the sidings incorporated parts of the old loop. Hitherto in the summer, drivers had experienced difficulty in edging around the loop when crowds thronged the ferry approaches; now conductors struggled to turn the trolleys as passengers clambered off one end whilst others pushed on board at the other. Point boys assisted car movements, temporary staff sold tickets to the waiting crowds and an inspector was always on duty in summer. In winter only the pair of sidings nearest the Ferry Hotel was used, but in the summer the Seabank Road cars used the northern pair.

From the same date, 29 March 1907, the flow in and out of New Brighton was reversed, with inbound cars travelling via Virginia Road and outbound via Victoria Road (in response of an incident in May 1905 when a Seabank Road car brakes failed, left the track and crashed into the North and South Wales Bank on the corner of Rowson Street). To counter local opposition to the reversed flow, Travers unsuccessfully explored the possibility of doubling the track in Victoria Road. The 1904 Bill, had it succeeded, would have provided a 90-yard storage siding in Virginia Road and a one-way avoiding line from Victoria Road via Grosvenor Road and Egerton Street to rejoin Rowson Street, but Greene had opposed this, claiming that outbound cars would lose potential traffic by not passing through the main junction.

Further track improvements were made at the busy Rowson Street/Victoria Road junction in 1911. The single track at the foot of Rowson Street hill was doubled and a new crossover installed at Pickering Road. This was used by early morning cars which arrived from the depot via Warren Drive, reversed in lower part of Rowson Street and then proceeded down the wrong track to the crossover. A Collins' automatic point controller was installed for outbound cars in Victoria Road for a three-month trial; if the driver wished to alter the setting, he went under the skate with the power on. Similar equipment was provided at Molyneux Drive, Brighton Street (Church Street) and Liscard Village in 1912 and in the following year at Seacombe Ferry and the top of Falkland Road. In February 1912 the track was doubled between St James Vicarage and Atherton Street (Victoria Road) leaving a short length of single line immediately prior to the junction. The proximity of the Wirral Railway cutting at New Brighton station and the excessive camber of the road prevented any further extension of the double track.

A further improvement at New Brighton did not materialise. As part of a campaign to create a resort to rival Blackpool and

Southport, the Council was determined to improve New Brighton's image. The 1906 Improvement Act had sanctioned a stretch of promenade linking the pier approach with a new Marine Park. In the process many of the old buildings near the ferry pier were swept away, including the notorious Ham and Eggs Parade, a collection of seedy cafes and amusement arcades. The New Brighton Improvements Association recommended the construction of a double track tramway along the new promenade at a cost of £8,000, but due to the short distance and the seasonal nature of the traffic the Council refused. However, by 1913 they were again considering an application to Parliament for powers to build a line linking New Brighton with Harrison Drive/Grove Road, to be operated in the summer months by toast rack cars, partly on private track across the sand dunes, unfortunately the war intervened and the idea was never revived.

By 7 February 1911 double track had also been laid in Wheatland Lane between Geneva Road and Milton Road, and in April 1912 along Warren Drive from a point north of Ennerdale Road down to Grove Road Junction. Attention then turned to the Seabank Road route. The most heavily used stretch of single track and loops on the system, from Molyneux Drive to Manor Road, was re-laid in stages between March 1914 and March 1915, including some road widening and renewing the feeder cables and the overhead. A passenger shelter was also provided at Manor Road. A siding in either Manor Road or Trafalgar Road for cars awaiting cinema crowds was rejected, a second crossover being installed in King Street about 15 yards south of the existing one. To prevent wheel screech and reduce wear on sharp-curves, track fountain hydrants were fitted in 1911 at Hose Side Road, Grove Road (Warren Drive) and Victoria Road (Rowson Street).

The Urban District of Wallasey became a Municipal Borough in 1910 and a County Borough three years later. The word "Council" was swiftly replaced by "Corporation" on the rocker panels of the cars, and the new coat of arms were applied, though some cars are thought to have retained the WCT monogram until after World War I. The population had risen rapidly by 25,000 to 78,000 during the ten years 1900-10 and by 1913 had reached 83,000, due in no small part to the joint role played by the trams and the ferries.

New Brighton Lifeboat

The Lancaster Gazette, Saturday 20th October, 1821

Several lifeboats, of very large dimensions, and constructed on different principles, are, we understand, now building at Liverpool, to be stationed on the adjacent coast. One of them, we have heard, will be stationed at Wallasey.24

---

24 The Lancaster Gazette, Saturday 20th October, 1821

New Brighton Lifeboat Station has a remarkable history of bravery with 48 awards for gallantry. The station is one of four lifeboat stations that operate an inshore hovercraft alongside the conventional lifeboat. The awards history is as follows:

1851 Silver Medals were awarded to Coxswains Peter Cropper, Thomas Evans and Joseph Formby for their long service on the Liverpool Dock Trustees lifeboat.

1863 The RNLI established a lifeboat station and the tubular lifeboat were kept on moorings in the River Mersey.

Silver Medals were awarded to Coxswain Thomas Evans, Thomas Evans Junior and William Evans for their efforts in rescuing 55 people from the stranded *John H Elliot*.

1870 A Silver Medal was awarded to Coxswain Richard Thomas for rescuing two people from the schooner *Elephant* on 19 October 1869. He had jumped aboard and rescued one man from the rigging as it crashed over the side.

1877 A Silver Medal was awarded to Hiram Linaker for 'his long and intrepid services'.

1883 In heavy seas Crew Member Charles Finlay was washed out of the lifeboat and drowned.

1893 The steam lifeboat *Duke of Northumberland* was placed on service.

1894 A Silver Medal was awarded to Coxswain William Martin for his 'gallant services'.

1905 Crew Members Allan Dodd and John Jones, acting as night watchmen, died from the fumes from a fire they had lit to keep themselves warm.

1923 Crew Member WJ Liversage died as a result of exposure on a lifeboat service.

The station's first motor lifeboat was placed on service.

1925 Assistant Mechanic Herbert Harrison drowned after he was thrown out of the boarding boat.

1928 A Silver Medal was awarded to Coxswain George Robinson and Bronze Medals to Crew Members John Nicholson, George Carmody, Ralph Scott, Wilfred Garbutt, Samuel Jones, William Liversage, and John Moore for rescuing 24 men from the steamer *Emile Delmas*.

1938 A Silver Medal was awarded to Coxswain W Jones and Bronze Medals to Second Coxswain J Nicholson, Mechanic W Garbutt and Second Mechanic J Mason for rescuing three men from the fishing boat *Progress* and four men from the schooner

Loch Ranza Castle that was drifting towards shore on 23 November 1938.

1947 A Bronze Medal was awarded to Second Coxswain WS Jones for evacuating the crew of six from a fort in the River Mersey.

1950 A Bronze Medal was awarded to Acting Coxswain William S Jones for rescuing four people from the schooner *Happy Harry*.

1954 A motor boarding boat was provided for the station from the proceeds of Panto Day, an annual event organised by Liverpool University students; it was named *Panto*.

1957 A Bronze Medal was awarded to Coxswain George Stonall for rescuing the crew from the coaster *J B Kee*.

1962 Second Mechanic FK Neilson lost his life on 6 March when he fell overboard from the boarding boat while approaching the lifeboat.

1963 A Centenary Vellum was awarded to the station.

1973 The all weather lifeboat was withdrawn from service and the station became an inshore lifeboat (ILB) station. An Atlantic 21 B class lifeboat became operational on 19 May.

1974 Silver Medals were awarded to Coxswain Edward Brown and Crew Member Robin Middleton, and Thanks of the Institution Inscribed on Vellum to Crew Members Clifford Downing, Alan Boult and Ian Campbell for rescuing three men from the fishing vessel *E B H*.

1975 The figure of 100,000 people rescued by the RNLI was reached when the ILB rescued a 13-year-old boy from a rubber

143

dinghy. A Framed certificate to mark the occasion was presented by the boy, Stuart Nixon, to the station.

1976 The Thanks of the Institution Inscribed on Vellum was awarded to Helmsman Edward B Brown for a search for the yacht *Annalivia*.

1982 A Bronze Medal was awarded to Helmsman Edward B Brown and the Thanks of the Institution Inscribed on Vellum to Crew Member Michael Jones for rescuing two crew from the yacht *Ocea*.

1988 The Thanks of the Institution Inscribed on Vellum was awarded to Helmsman Anthony Clare and Framed Letters of Thanks to Crew Members Geoffrey Prince and Anthony Jones for rescuing the three crew from the yacht *Samsal* on 6 October 1987. The crew were also awarded the Ralph Glister Award for the most meritorious service carried out in a lifeboat less than 10 metres in 1987.

1990 A new boathouse was built for the Atlantic 21 lifeboat and launching tractor and also provided a souvenir sales outlet and improved crew facilities.

1994 The following awards were made after a car had plunged through the railings at Egremont: Thanks of the Institution Inscribed on Vellum to Crew Members Michael Jones and Tony Clare; Framed Letters of Thanks to Crew Members Neil Jones and Barry Shillinglaw and Shore Helper Tony Jones.

1995 For landing and resuscitating an unconscious man in rough seas the following awards were made: The Thanks of the Institution Inscribed on Vellum to Helmsman Michael Jones; Framed Letters of Thanks to Crew Members Howard Jones, Neil

Jones and Michael Haxby, and the crew of the private rescue service boat *County Rescue,* Richard Finlay and John Goodwin.

1996 An Atlantic 75 lifeboat, B-721 *Rock Light*, named after the lighthouse at the entrance to the River Mersey, was placed on service on 9 January.

Life-Boat at New Brighton.

2000 After an unconscious man was recovered from the sea early on Christmas morning 1999 the Thanks of the Institution Inscribed on Vellum was awarded to Helmsman Michael Jones for helming the lifeboat at the very limit of the operational capabilities of a B class lifeboat. A collective Framed Letter of Thanks was awarded to Crew Members Barry Shillinglaw, Paul Wright and Howard Jones. Eight shore helpers received a collective Letter of Appreciation from the Director, and the Station Honorary Secretary received a Letter of Appreciation from the Chief of Operations.

2005 The inshore rescue hovercraft, H-005 *Hurley Spirit*, was placed on service. This is the RNLI's fifth hovercraft and was donated by Mrs Kay Hurley MBE. The hovercraft works alongside the ILB covering the many areas around the coastline where a conventional lifeboat cannot operate.

2007 Lifeboat Press Officer Philip Hockey was awarded the MBE in the Queen's Birthday Honours.

Housing

Wellington Road Villas

In the early years of the 19th Century, Wallasey, then consisting of the Townships of Liscard, Poulton-cum-Seacombe and Wallasey, was populated principally by people who earned their living in rural occupation, mainly agriculture, and apart from such places as Leasowe Castle, Poulton Hall and Liscard Manor House, there were few large residences to be found. In 1832 James Atherton, a retired Liverpool merchant who had already emerged successfully from several property speculations on the Liverpool side of the river, and his son-in-law, William Rowson, a Prescot Solicitor, entered into an agreement to purchase 140 acres of sand hills and heath land from John Penkett, Lord of the Manor of Liscard, for £23,000, in what was later to become New Brighton, and proceeded to level the area on the basis that every house built would be the possessor of a good sea-view and be surrounded by ample grounds. As a result, during the next few years, roads such as Wellington Road, Montpellier Crescent and St. George's Mount, which still exist to some extent in their original state, came into being, and large houses began to spring up in the more outlying parts of the district as Liverpool cotton brokers, ship-owners and merchants awoke to the realisation of the natural attractions of that particular part of the Wirral Peninsula. Many of those houses have since disappeared and left no pictorial record behind them, but fortunately there are some instances where either the building, although converted to other uses, are still standing, or demolition has taken place sufficiently recently for photographs to be available. Enough evidence has survived, however, to indicate why, in earlier days, Wallasey earned the title of "the bedroom of Liverpool", a distinction which, to lesser degree, it still retains. 25

---

25 J.S Rebecca

148

In the Wallasey of the 19th Century there were several large landowners to be found, and as their names crop up from time to time in telling the stories of Mansions of Wallasey, it might be helpful if they are mentioned now. Apart from those already mentioned, the two largest were probably Sir John Tobin, of Liscard Hall, who made considerable speculative purchases of land, notably in what is now the docks area, and John Ashley Marsden, a brush manufacturer, of Liscard Castle, who practice appears to have been to buy up various estates in the district with mortgage assistance, develop then if necessary, and then let them. He had fingers in many pies, but after his death in 1853 the properties were sold off, in some cases to existing tenants. Other landowners to a lesser degree were John North, of 'Stonebark', Warren Drive, John Davies, also an Attorney, who lived originally in Liverpool and later at 'Hoseside Farm' and the Holland family of 'Liscard Vale House'.

Cliff Villa

In 1833 land was up for sale for the building of villas. The first was built by William Rowson. In 1836 William paid £996. 2/- for six parcels of land at the west end of the estate, measuring in total 34,000 square yards. Here he built the house 'Cliff Villa'. It was a single storey house with a brick design and a stucco finish. The design of the property was based on 'Longwood House', where Napoleon lived whilst exiled on St. Helena. William died in 1863 and his wife a year later. As there was no children the house was passed on by his will to his nephew, Mr G Rowson Berry, and he remained living at 'Cliff Villa' until his death in 1874.

The estate went through various hands until the Corporation purchased 'Cliff Villa' for £9,000 in 1926 who established an aquarium. In 1931, the Guide Dogs for the Blind Committee held a meeting at the house and in 1934 the 'Guide Dogs for the Blind

Association' was formed. They were allowed the use of a single room by the Corporation but soon afterwards the whole of the house and grounds were made available to them and they remained there until the outbreak of World War II when the army moved in.

The house received heavy damage in an air raid and was subsequently demolished in 1960. As is generally known, the two large blocks of flats now standing in the grounds are known as 'The Cliff'.

Rock Villla

In 1837 William Rowson sold off one of his portions of land, amounting to 2,120 square miles and adjacent to 'Cliff Villa', to Peter Greenall, Brewer, of St Helens. It is not known if Rowson or Greenall built this house on the land but right from the start it was known as 'Rock Villa' and it is, of course, still standing today. Peter Greenall used the house as a summer residence. His grandfather was Thomas Greenall, who founded 'Greenall Whitley's St. Helens Brewery ' in 1762. Peter married Eleanor Pilkington in 1821 who was the daughter of Dr William Pilkington.

In 1826 Peter formed a partnership with William Pilkington and formed 'St Helen's Crown Glass Company', now known as 'Pilkington's Group'. Due to commitments to the brewery Peter was forced to sell his shares in 1839.

On the 18th September 1845 Peter Greenall died of a stroke. He was commemorated by naming a street after him but later it was renamed as Alexandra Road.

The property was occupied by a variety of tenants but in 1875 marked the arrival of the Peers Family, more notably James Peers (1816-1886), who was a Cotton-Broker. His son, George Hunter

Peers (1846-1914), was later to persuade the local board to purchase Central Park after the death of Harold Littledale in 1889. George also went on to demolish the mill on the Breck and replacing it with a residence which was well known for eighty years as 'Millthwaite'.

The reign of the Peers family at 'Rock Villa' ended after the finish of the First World War. The next occupant being Mr C.R Marples, a Cotton-Broker, who lived there for some years to be followed by Pat Ahern, a Wallasey commission agent, and then the Wallasey Sea Cadets, who made the house as their headquarters for awhile, In 1959 'Rock Villa' was purchased by the architect Mr Norman Kingdom which included the caves under the dwelling which were formed out of the soft stone of the Red and Yellow Noses. Access to these caves, which still exist, was from the shore but the promenade was built so blocking the entrance. The caves can only be accessed via a manhole in the 'Rock Villa' garden.

The house itself originally had gothic features but owing to past neglect and some war damage all of these have been lost and replaced with more modern styles which have altered its character.

Ewart Villas

Still standing today next to 'Rock Villa' are 2 large semi-detached houses, officially known as 'Ewart Villas', and now numbered 50, 52 and 54 Wellington Road but which have borne various other names during their lives, such as 'Turf Moor', 'Brodawel', 'The Rocks', 'Yellow Nose House', 'Lyndhurst' and so on. There were many occupants over the years; one of the better known was William Rathbone VI (1819 - 1902) who lived in one of the houses in the 1860's. He used the villa as a summer residence as his main home was 'Greenbank' in Sefton Park, Liverpool. William was a partner in the great Liverpool business-house of Rathbone Bros & Co and its associated firm of grain merchants Ross T.Smyth & Co, both still in business today.

The care of his dying first wife in 1859, Lucretia, by a nurse, prompted him to campaign for a system of district nursing to enable the poor to benefit from similar care. The involvement of Florence Nightingale led to a close friendship. In 1862, the Liverpool Training School and Home for Nurses was established, from which basis a district nursing system was implemented in Liverpool through the 1860s and spread throughout the country. His involvement with this scheme also made him aware of the poor state of the workhouse hospitals, and he did much to assist in the reform of nursing in workhouses.

William Rathbone died in 1902 at the age of 83. William's daughter, Eleanor Rathbone, born in 1872, was the famous social worker and Member of Parliament for the independent party 'Combined Universities' from 1929 until her death in 1946. There have been owners of the villas but overall the buildings have hardly changed in the past 160 years apart from one or two windows. The west half of the villas has today been divided into two dwellings and the east half is now in use as a Nursing Home.

Ewart House

As part of the transaction entered into with John Penkett in 1832, James Atherton purchased for his own use approximately 9,000 square yards of land in 1836. At the corner of Wellington Road and Portland Street, and on it built himself a dwelling. The house was not the most attractive building. It was built in ashlar in an Italianate style with an asymmetrical plan. The house had moulded string courses denoting floor levels, canopies with brackets over the window openings which had a small panel sash frames and an unimposing front entrance. When viewed from Wellington Road

152

the house was two storeys high with a single storey side extension and with a small off centre section rising to a third floor which gave access on to a flat roof having a pierced balustrade. It seemed to be built in "steps and stairs". The seaward elevation fared no better having a stepped front with the most projecting sections adored with a large bay window. For the founder of New Brighton and the developer of Everton it could have been more appealing.

One of the problems of the site was the contours of the rock formation which could have poised difficulties with the layout of the dwelling but not affect the look of it. These difficulties presented themselves again when the site was demolished 100 years later.

There is some doubt as to the original name of the building, but two years later, in 1838, James Atherton died, leaving the property to his widow, Elizabeth, who the following year sold it to James Christopher Ewart, partner in a prosperous Liverpool firm of merchants, 'Ewart, Myers & Co', he renamed the house 'Ewart House'. A title which remained until 1934.

Joseph Ewart's father, William Ewart, was a long time friend of John Gladstone. When John Gladstone's wife had their fourth son he christened the child 'William Ewart Gladstone' as a tribute to his father's great friend. William Ewart Gladstone subsequently became Prime Minister.

Joseph died on the 12th December 1868 at the age of 68 when he succumbed to fever.

Clifton Villa

History of 'Clifton Villa' on the west side of 'Walmer Villa' is rather obscure, although it would seem that as far back as 1853 a Mr Charles Beamish was living there. 20 years later the occupant was William Chadburn, then described as an optician but better known since as the founder of Chadburn's Ship Telegraph Co. Ltd whose products must have travelled the seven seas many times. At the beginning of the 20th Century Mr F.H Chambers, a well known ship-owner, had arrived on the scene, to be succeeded after a few years by a variety of occupants, including Colonel Myles Emmet Byrne, John M. Union, an accountant and eventually in 1946 the Misses Jessie and Frances Stoner and so on.

Portland Villa

Another house on Wellington Road that has continued without change of name is 'Portland Villa', originally one of the homes of Adam Dugdale, a Liverpool Cotton Broker, who had warehouses in Piccadilly and Moseley Street, Manchester. His main residence was 'Dovecot House' in Knotty Ash, Liverpool, then a pleasant mansion standing in parkland at the corner of Pilch Lane and Prescot Road, but now replaced by a sprawling Corporation estate bearing the same name. The connection with New Brighton began in January 1835 when he purchased a plot of land, 2,013 square yards in extent from James Atherton and William Rowson, at a cost of £704.11/- or 2/1d per square yard. Two houses must have been built on the land almost immediately, as in March 1837 Dugdale sold one of the houses to and 995 1/4 square yards of land to Dr Thomas Raffles, the famous Liverpool Divine. Dr Raffles, then minister of Great George Street Congregational Church, named his house 'Stamford Villa', after his illustrious cousin, Sir Stamford Raffles, the founder of Singapore but it is probable that, like Dugdale, he too retained his Liverpool residence at 28, Mason Street, Edge Lane, then a fashionable quarter. Adam Dugdale died on 8th April 1838, leaving the property to three nephews, the sons of his brother Nathaniel, and the house finally passed out of the Dugdale family in 1857, when it was sold to Peter Joynson Jr, a cotton broker and son of Thomas Joynson, of 'Longview House' Seaview Road, for £1,450.

Peter Joynson remained at 'Portland Villa' until approximately 1874, when he appears to have been made bankrupt, and his property was then sold by his mortgagers, the Liverpool Commercial Banking company, to a Mr R.J Walsh for £2,400. Walsh remained there until his death in 1895, and the following year the house was purchased for £2,175 by the Thornton family, a well known building contractor in a large way off business in Liverpool, who spent over fifty years living there before moving on.

When the Thornton family left 'Portland Villa' the house came on the market again and was resold in 1965 for division into two dwellings. The accommodation was divided vertically quite easily and so becoming 42 and 42a Wellington Road.

Redcliffe Villa

In 1845, on land purchased from William Rowson, 'Redcliffe' was built to the order of Daniel Nielson, a well known Liverpool stockbroker, from designs prepared by Harvey Lonsdale Elmes. Elmes achieved fame as the architect of St. Georges Hall, Liverpool, although he died at an early age before the building was completed. 'Redcliffe' is built in red ashlar sandstone in the Tudor style but unfortunately over the years the exterior has been mutilated by various alterations, with modern windows and extensions. By 1851 Nielson had been replaced by William Hughes Daunt, an Iron Merchant, who, like his predecessor was a worshipper at St. Hilary's Church. The Parish Register show that between 1850 and 1865 the Daunts had no fewer than 11 children baptised at the church, it is perhaps not surprising that the family vault is one of the largest in the Churchyard.

After the Daunts had left 'Redcliffe', there were a variety of occupants including the Locket family who owned land where Trafalgar Road is today. The Lockets were followed by Colonel

155

Henry Langdon, of the well known Liverpool tent making firm, who spent nearly fifteen years there and in about 1925 he was succeeded by Mr C. Graham, a Liverpool merchant, who ten years later turned the home into a hotel.

After 1957/58 the building came up for sale again and an auction was held on the premises but the building failed to reach a reserve of £1,750. However, after the sale, a private negotiation was pursued and 'Redcliffe' was finally sold to Mr Walter Farrell, a well known local builder and roofer who converted the property into flats making his home in one of the ground floor apartments.

Swiss Villas

Numbers 28 and 30 Wellington Road is a pair of identical houses with an addition having been made to Number 28 on the East side with a whole section having been built over the side garden. These two dwellings form a long Gothic group, stucco rendered and painted with fancy bargeboards, ornamented chimneys, drop moulds over the pointed arched windows and to the seaward side having cast iron balconies and spiral stairs down to the gardens facing the sea. These dwellings started life in 1838, and appear to have been known as 'Swiss Villas'. In the absence of any details in the street directories of those days, it is difficult to know who were the first owners, although it would seem that it could well have been the respective builders Messrs Richard and Paul Baker for Number 28 and Messrs Westmore and Crosby for Number 30.

Swiss Cottage

A Mr. William Hadfield, a Liverpool Merchant, is shown on the Tithe Map of 1841 as being the occupant of Number 30 which by then had become known as 'Swiss Cottage' so retaining part of the original name from then onwards. Number 28 changes its name completely. Early details of successive occupants are scarce, but one person. Mr James Kiernan, who went there in the early years of the last century, qualifies for special mention. Apart from being a Councillor, he was very much involved in the entertainment world, having joined the staff of the old Rotunda Theatre in Liverpool in 1875 as a check-taker, at a weekly wage of 9/-. He left there in 1886 to open the Westminster Theatre in Walton, and subsequently the Paddington Theatre, the Tivoli Palace, the Kursaal, Liverpool, the Empire Theatre, Barnsley, the Olympia Cinema, the Park Palace and the Sefton Palace. He was concerned with the 'Irving Theatre, Borough Road, Seacombe but by 1913 he had retired. After his departure from 'Swiss Cottage', Mr W. Esplen, a well known Liverpool ship-owner, spent several years at the house, but around 1925 conversion to flats appears to have taken place.

<u>Warwick Villa</u>

This house, standing on the west corner of Wellington Road and Atherton Street, is known as 'Warwick Villa', and has retained its name throughout its life, though on some deeds it appears as 'Warwick Cottage'. Sold by William Rowson to a Mr Isaac Harrop in 1844, it seems to have changed its occupants with great regularity every decade or so, with the result that a variety of Merchants, Solicitors, Stockbrokers and so on all called it home at one time or another. Mr Sandie, a Soap Manufacturer, who afterwards lived at 'Mosslands', the mansion that use to stand at the corner of Breck Road and the Bidston footpath, lived at the turn of the last century, in the days when it was quite usual, particularly after a gale, to find sand drifting up to the back door.

'Warwick Cottage' is one of the several houses in Wellington Road which present a single storey frontage on the landward entrance side and two storey's to the seaward side, this being due to the fall in land from Wellington Road to the shore. The dwelling is classical is style, the most attractive side that facing the sea, whilst the other elevation appears to have had the bays added at some later date and are more Gothic, this fact confirmed by repair work. There is a strong possibility that 'Warwick Cottage' was designed by the same architecture for 'Redcliffe' and 'Ellerslie', that being Harvey Lonsdale Elmes.

Mr Sandie was followed by Joseph William Roby a Solicitor who died on July 23rd 1912 when the property passed to Mr Henry Chester Jones. Mr Jones was a Corn Miller with offices in Fenwick Street, Liverpool and he stayed quite some time at this villa living here from 1912 until early 1936 when he dies on 1st April of that year. He was followed by Edward Ellison Knowles, otherwise Edward Ellison, a Master Stevedore of 7 Corfe Buildings, Preesons Row, Liverpool and 1 Rock Park, Birkenhead. Edward Knowles remained in possession, but not living there, from 1936 to 1950, when it passed to Elizabeth Ellen Ellison, his widow, and eventually to his son also named Edward Knowles. The son was also a Stevedore and had a company known as The Liverpool Derricking and Carrying Company Ltd. He sold out to Mr and Mrs Hockey in 1961.

Close by to this dwelling is the Winter Gardens Theatre which was, in early days a very successful venue, and rumour has it that Lawrence Irving, the actor son of an even more famous actor father, Sir Henry Irving, stayed here with his actress wife Mabel Hackney when performing at the theatre. Sadly they both lost their lives as passengers when the 'Empress of Ireland' was in collision with another vessel, the 'Storstadt', on May 29th 1914 off Quebec. 1, 1012 people were drowned, including the Irving's.

'Warwick Cottage' is presently converted, with minimum alterations internally and no alterations externally, to three flats. Due to neglect over the initial years the original cast iron railings to Wellington Road, beyond repair, had been replaced with an exact replica, the moulds having been made using some of the better parts of the originals. It is interesting to note that the gateway to these railings (now listed) is not the same as the original; the new cast iron gateway came from the Guinea Gap Baths in Seacombe and was situated at the entrance by the pay office between the two turnstiles. The gate complete with the turnstile supports were purchased and saved by Mr P. Hockey when the Guinea Gap Baths were modernised, and erected at 'Warwick Cottage'.

The upper garden facing Wellington Road, when it was first laid out had a cast iron peach house with hot water heating pipes and the gardens facing the sea had two very long greenhouses also in cast iron and heated from a main boiler. These greenhouses, now completely gone, had fig trees and other Victorian delights. All the soil, of course, had to be imported as sand was the base and it must have been disheartening gardening in this positioning and fighting against drifting sand in adverse weather conditions.

Some Property Prices in the 19th Century

Liverpool Mercury, Thursday, May 18th, 1899

To be let – Unfurnished Houses

New Brighton – 3, Mount Pleasant Road. £30 per annum.

New Brighton – No. 1 Mount Road, Upper Brighton. Semi-detached; drawing, dining, and breakfast rooms; five bedrooms; kitchens on ground floor; washing kitchen, larder, wine cellar, butler's pantry, bath, w.c, hot and cold water; gardens back and front; rent £45. Key at 25, Mount Road – N.B. – Has splendid and uninterrupted views over Wallasey; the Welsh mountains, and the Great Orme's Head. – Apply to John Hughes, 14. Tower

Buildings, Old Churchyard.26

New Brighton – 53, Meadow Street. Rent £20.

New Brighton – St. George's Mount – "WOODCOTE'; three entertaining rooms, seven bedrooms, &c; sheltered and healthy situation; pleasant view front and back. Apply next door.

New Brighton – No. 1, Pickering Road; contains breakfast room, two parlours, five bedrooms, kitchen, and several pantries; rent £40. – Apply to W. And J. Venmore, 200, Scotland Road, Liverpool.

New Brighton – 4, Prescott Street, - Large SHOP, with excellent windows, suitable for grocers, draper's, or other business; surrounded by increasing residential houses; good opening for a branch establishment; house attached. Key at No. 8 – W.E. Nelson, 22 Lord Street. Telephone 5876.

Liscard Vale House

In the last century there existed an attractive residential area known as 'Liscard Vale', in part of which Vale Park is now situated. It boasted several smaller houses and two mansions, one of which, known as 'Liscard Vale House' for many years, still survives, and for some time duly as a cafe for visitors to the park. An early occupant and possibly its builder, was Richard Bateson, a Cotton Broker, who subsequently moved to 'Newland House' in Wallasey Road, but in 1844 the property was purchased by Charles Holland, a Liverpool Merchant, who had previously been living at 'West

26 Liverpool Mercury, Thursday, May 18th, 1899

160

Bank'. a large house standing in its own grounds at what is now the corner of Egerton Street and the Promenade. That house is no longer in existence, but is commemorated by West Bank Avenue off Magazine Lane.

'Liscard Vale House' when first built, was much smaller that it appears today and if care is taken to view the building one can easily see the original dwelling before it was enlarged. The early house is seen on the left hand side in a regency style character of tasteful proportions. It was a very nice looking house but when Charles Holland purchased the property it was too small for his family, he had nine children, so he enlarged it and added the Victorian exterior.

Charles Holland was an offshoot of a well known family which is said to have originated at Up Holland, Lancashire, in the 13th Century, and was later to be found at Sandle Bridges, near Knutsford. His parents were Samuel Holland, a prosperous merchant living at No.126 Duke Street, Liverpool, then a fashionable residential area, and his wife Catherine, daughter of John Menzies, a Liverpool Accountant, while his own wife was Elizabeth Gaskell, daughter of a Warrington sail-canvas manufacturer. She was well known locally for her readings at the old Egremont Institute on Tobin Street, a centre of culture in those days, and her brother William, a Unitarian Minister and Professor of English Literature in Manchester, provided her with an illustrious sister-in-law, in as much in 1832 he married Elizabeth Cleghorn Stevenson, better known as "Mrs Gaskell", the authoress of "Cranford", "Mary Barton" and other works, and biographer of Charlotte Bronte. As Mrs Gaskell's mother was a Holland of Sandle Bridge, who had married Thomas Stevenson, Keeper of the Treasury Records, and taken up residence in Chelsea, Mrs Gaskell was also a cousin of Charles Holland. Another cousin was Henry Holland, who spent a brief period in business in Liverpool, later

161

studied medicine in Edinburgh, and after commencing practice in London in 1816, was subsequently appointed Physician to Queen Victoria. He was created a Baronet in 1853, and his eldest son eventually became Viscount Knutsford.

Returning to 'Liscard Vale House'. In 1866 Charles Holland purchased a large piece of land on the seaward side of Grove Road from the Trustees of John S. Davies, deceased, late of 'Hoseside Farm', for £8,000. and the following year sold 17,000 square yards of this land to Major James Walter, of 'Verulam Lodge', better known as 'The Grange', for £1,340, to enable Major Walter to extend his grounds to Jockey Lane, as it was then called, but today known as Sandcliffe Road. Charles Holland, who had become a Justice of the Peace for the Wirral, died in 1870, but a year later the Trustees of his estate purchased a further 25,500 square yards of land in this area from a Mr Stanley Sutton, at a cost of £1,550. The year 1888, however, saw the construction of the Seacombe, Hoylake and Deeside Railway, and to enable that track to be taken through to New Brighton the Holland Trustees sold off 10,888 square yards of this land to the Railway Company, for £2,272. Mrs Holland, Charles widow, died in 1892, and in 1898 the remaining Trustees and her own Executors entered into an agreement for the sale of 'Liscard Vale House' and its grounds to a Mr David Beano Rappart, for a total of £7,000. Five months later Mr Rappart arranged to resell the estate to Wallasey Urban District for £7.750, and the deal was concluded in November, 1898. Finally to complete the picture as far as the Hollands were concerned, Charles Holland's Trustees sold thirty-one acres of the Grove Road land, including four acres on the other side of the railway, to the Urban District council in 1909, for £15,500, and a year later the Municipal Golf Links was established.

The Woodlands

Just to the north of 'Liscard Vale House' stood a larger mansion, which appears to have been known as 'Liscard Vale Hall' initially, but later to become 'The Woodlands', possibly to avoid confusion with 'Liscard Vale House'. The property was built at first more in the style of a comfortable country mansion. It appears to have been changed later on, or "modernised" by the substitution of the small paned windows for large sash windows, the addition of two two storey bays, a dormer window to the roof and the increased height of all the chimneys, necessitated no doubt by the down draught caused by the nearby trees.

Owing to lack of information in the Directories, the chain of ownership becomes a little involved, but Henry Binns, a Cotton Broker, was one of the earliest residents, to be followed by his son-in-law, Henry Ellythorp Robson, also a Cotton Broker, in 1850. In the 1870's both Alderman James Smith, later of 'Dalmorton House', and his brother Samuel Smith, the M.P, later of "Clifton Hall', are shown as being in occupation, but by 1880 R.A Eskrigge, son-in-law and partner of the Mr H.E Robson previously mentioned, had moved in from 'Fir Cottage', Magazine Lane, and remained there for many years. In 1898 the house and approximately 13,000 square yards of land were purchased by the Urban District Council, at a cost of £3,500, from the Trustees of the late H.E Robson, and added to 'Liscard Vale House' to form Vale Park. The right to continue its residence at 'The Woodlands' was reserved to Mr Eskrigge and his wife for a minimum of six years and after their occupation the house was eventually demolished.

There are paintings of 'The Woodlands' and its surroundings by members of the Robson family, portraying what must have been a delightful spot in the old days, well-wooded with river views and grounds running right down to the river. The promenade had not then been built, and Mr Robson laid his own pathway along the shore to New Brighton Ferry.

Theatre & Cinema

New Brighton Floral Pavilion

In its heyday New Brighton was the accepted rendezvous for theatre goers and with seven theatres, was rich in live entertainment. From the 1890's to the outbreak of World War Two and shortly afterwards, hundreds of top stars trod the boards and enthusiastic audiences filled the seats of The Tivoli, Winter Gardens, Tower Theatre, Pier Pavilion, Palace Theatre and the Victoria Gardens Pavilion. Over the years these wonderful theatres, one by one, shut their doors. In 2006 the Floral was facing a similar fate.

Determined to keep the dream alive, the theatre management embarked on an ambitious development campaign that has revived this majestic venue to her former glory. Though she may look different to when she opened her doors in 1913, the magic and charm that has prevailed over nearly a century is evident as you walk through the new doors. Rebuilt as part of an exciting regeneration programme for 'Brand New Brighton', the Floral is living proof of the power of live entertainment in uniting communities through culture.

167

The Picture above is how the Floral Pavilion now looks today following a new and modern building being erected on the site. The theatre closed in 2007 and was demolished as part of the town's £60 million Neptune Project redevelopment plans. The building was rebuilt to a new design and reopened in December 2008. The first act to perform at the venue after reopening was Ken Dodd, who has had a long association with the Floral Pavilion, making his first appearance in 1940. As well as an enlarged theatre auditorium, seating over 800, the complex also provides for conference facilities and a large multi-purpose lounge area.

The Tivoli Theatre

Boating Pool, New Brighton

This legendary theatre stood at New Brighton for only 40 years but in that short space of time was host to many famous acts from around the world. When the theatre was opened in 1914 New Brighton was already renowned for entertainment and as such the Tivoli Theatre had to fend off rivals such as the Tower Theatre and the Winter Gardens Theatre. To do this the company who ran the Tivoli hired Fred Ross who had previously been responsible for the success of the Tower Theatre, and hoping to follow suit; they in turn hired him. Ross helped bring many famous names to the theatre over the following decade and the theatre was an outstanding success.

The theatre closed in 1955 and remained derelict for some time before vandal managed to break in and cause a fire. The extent of the damaged was so great that the structure was deemed unsafe and it was demolished several days later.

The Palace Theatre

historyofwallasey.co.uk | Palace Theatre, 1906

In 1881 a new amusement complex opened on the Promenade which housed a grand hall, a small concert hall, skating rink aquarium and aviary. The main entrance was in Virginia Road with additional access from the Promenade. In 1893 the theatre became known as 'The Palace and Pavilion Theatre' and in 1895 it came under the control of the New Brighton Palace Company Ltd., with Mr. M.D. Ellery as Managing Director.

The fortunes of the enterprise changed with the arrival of the Tower and the Palace began to decline. Plans were developed to revitalise the Palace which involved a Manchester concern which proposed erecting the biggest revolving wheel the world had ever seen with forty-two carriages each holding forty passengers. However, the project was abandoned.

In 1906 the Palace exploited the new influence of animated pictures and thus becoming the second in Wallasey to be used as a cinema. The premises then became controlled by Wallasey Corporation, with Messrs. Lievers and Bennet the new leases and Mr. Percy Penny the new manager. Northern Cinematograph

Trading Company provided motion pictures in the mixed programme.

The opening first film programme comprised: *The Great Thaw Trial* - the topic of the day; hundreds of side splitting comic pictures *My Word, if you 're not off* - the popular saying illustrated; *The Limerick Craze* - showing how Jones did not win £5,000; *The Model Husband* - a real side splitter; no wife should be without him; *The Gamekeepers Dog* - man's faithful friend in time of trouble; and *The Hits of the Season* - shots of His Majesty King Edward VII and all the Royal family aboard the battleship Dreadnought. Other early films included *The Fisher Girls Wooing. Satan at Play* and *The Mill Girl* (a touching tale of factory life). The films were considered to be of good technical quality and of such a moral and refined nature that ladies, gentlemen and children would find them pleasing. Performances were each evening at 8.00 pm with a Grand Illuminated Children's' Matinee on Saturday afternoons at 3.00 pm. Admission cost between 2d and 1/6 for the evening house and 2d and 3d for the children's' afternoon sessions.

Inside the Palace was however, was spartan, with its poor heating, corrugated iron roof and uncomfortable wooden bench on a flat ground floor. Originally there was seating for 750 which was later expanded by the addition of a balcony. Entering the cinema was by a small square vestibule that was on a level with the balcony and also which contained the pay box. On the right hand side of the vestibule was the staircase which led to the ground floor. The walls of the auditorium were plain with a deep painted dado and a high stage. The main decorative scheme was in off-white and crimson with two plaster statues of Greek goddesses in arched alcoves at either side of the stage. The stage used back cloth rollers instead of a fly tower.

In 1910 live shows became the main feature which was continued when Mr. F.Vaughan became manager. The Tivoli Company Ltd took control for awhile but when problems occurred with the building of the Tivoli the lease was then sold to Mr. Ludwig Blattner who was formerly with the Irving Theatre in Seacombe. To compete with the other more modern cinemas in the area the theatre underwent a new image and, after a short closure, was reopened as the 'Gaiety', on Easter Monday 1914. Modifications included an increased seating capacity to 1200 and the establishment of the Royal Bohemian Orchestra with Herr Heinrich Fieler and his violin.

Blattner's reign came to an abrupt end with the outbreak of the First World War in August 1914 and he was forced to take up residence in an internment camp for the duration. After the war Blattner was to become a film producer in London and also became well known as the inventor of a magnetic wire recorder known as the Blattnerphone. He died on October 1935 after committing suicide due to a failing business.

By October 1914, the "worked by an all-British staff" Gaiety was managed by Alfred Delmonte who later became the musical director at the Marina. He advertised the Gaiety with "numerous improvements -- including modern heating apparatus installed throughout the building" and claimed to be "the cosiest entertainment in the district". In December 1914 there was another change in administration and "beautiful pictures in conjunction with high-class orchestral music" were advertised with "Go-as-you-please" contests every Friday, the profits from the first week being donated to the Wallasey War Relief Fund.

Wounded soldiers from the front line attended Wednesday afternoon concerts at the Gaiety which became a regular feature as the war progressed. Artistes would give their time free of charge. The theatre was open for film performances for a period during the winter season but only on Wednesdays and Saturdays.

A major fire swept through the complex on 22nd April, 1916 which destroyed the skating rink and other parts of the building, but the theatre itself was saved as a result of the strenuous efforts of the firemen. For a time the theatre was known as 'Palace Picture Playhouse'. In 1920 the lease was taken over by Pat Collins Jnr who was a well-known fairground operator and the theatre then became known as 'Collins' Palace Cinema'. The main entertainment was films. But for a short period in 1923 there was a reversion to purely live shows when "the highest-class concert parties in the country" were advertised. The theatre closed throughout 1924-1925 and reopened on Whit Monday 1926 and advertised as redecorated and re-seated with prices ranging from 3d to 1/3. Joseph W.Gabriel was the lessee who was a well-known local pianist and conductor. Reginald Eysenck was the manager who was formerly of the Lyceum Picture House in Eastbourne.

Performances at the theatre included daily matinees at 2.30 pm and evening shows continuous from 6.15 pm to 10.15 pm. 'The Sky Raider' was the opening programme featuring Charles Nungesser (1892-1927) and Gladys Walton (1903-1993) with a Larry Semon Comedy. 'Frauds and Frenzies', 'Pathe Pictorial' and 'Pathe Gazette'. Plus a musical interlude by Joseph Gabriel and his orchestra.

On 11th December, 1926, the Palace finally closed, with a showing of 'Spook Ranch' featuring Hoot Gibson (1892-1962). Plans to develop the site were suggested in 1932 and after standing derelict for several years; the Palace was eventually demolished in 1933 to make way for the construction of The New Palace Amusement Park.

New Brighton Winter Gardens

In 1907 Messrs A. Douglas and H.E Jones leased the old Conservative Club in Atherton Street for Saturday evening concerts. In February 1908 the Alexandra Hall was renamed as the Winter Gardens with programmes of plays and films complete with an orchestra and palms. However, due to cramped conditions both on stage and in the dressing rooms, it was decided to rebuild the Winter Gardens and in 1910 the old auditorium was removed to be replaced by a grand circle. A 60 ft x 33 ft stage was provided as well as improved dressing rooms. Also installed, which was a wonder at the time, was electric lighting. The Winter Gardens remained opened throughout the First World War and in 1919, Mr Douglas became the sole owner.

In February, 1931 the directors decided to demolish the old Winter Gardens and build a new theatre in its place. Within four months the new theatre was rebuilt and opened on the 27th June, 1931. The new theatre was designed by Messrs T. Talisin Rees and R. Holt and had a striking facade with a canopy, displays boards, six entrances doors as well as floodlights for night time illuminations. The theatre could hold 1,400 seats.

The entrance foyer was large and housed the box office, two pay booths and a ladies' cloakroom; the gentlemen's cloak room was downstairs. On either side of the hall were stairs that led to a lounge with facilities for refreshments, including a bar. Above the mezzanine floor was a large balcony. An unusual feature of the balcony was the provision of two private boxes at either extremity of the circle front that curved outwards especially to accommodate them. Either side of the stage above each of the two exits there was an ornamental canopy supported by fibrous plaster columns. The main hall itself measured 87 ft 6 in x 57 ft 9 in. Beneath the balcony was a dome, illuminated by concealed lighting, whilst six groups of high-powered lights fitted with special reflectors in the ceiling void, provided the main illumination for the auditorium, the light passing through rectangular figured glass panels flush with the ceiling. The theatre boasted a large and well-equipped stage with fly-tower and generous dressing room facilities. The seats had arm rests and were of the tip-up variety.

From the time the Winter Gardens opened it was clear that its destiny was uncertain. The building was designed primarily as a theatre but with a projection room built on as an insurance resulting in a constant shift between live performances and film shows. The first year of opening was promising for the theatre but soon ran into trouble and takings slumped to £47 in one week. After reducing entrance charges and appealing for support the business survived. Stages productions however continued until the mid 1930's.

The Winter Gardens was taken over by Cheshire Picture Halls (later to become S.M. Super Cinemas) in 1936. Mr. Douglas remained as managing director. The most up-to-date projection apparatus was installed by the new owners - Western Electric Range Sound System, and a "short cinema season" was announced on 4th May, 1936, starting with 'The Passing of the Third Floor

Back' starring Conrad Veidt (1893-1943). However, within two weeks the cinema closed on 16th May for extensive modernisation which included the removal of the balcony boxes.

On 1st June 1936 the Winter Garden re-opened. Live performances again dominated the programme for the next few years. After war was declared in September 1939, the Government ordered all places of entertainment to close. Despite the order being revoked, from 15th September, the Winter Gardens remained closed. During the time a new cinema screen was installed as well as a RCA High Fidelity sound System and the new Kalee II film projectors. The Winter Gardens remained closed until 26th December, when a special Christmas production of 'Alice in Wonderland', with Donald Wolfit (1902-1968) was staged.

On 1st January 1940 the 'New Winter Gardens', thereafter known as, was given a grand opening with Alan Lusty at the Organ and a showing of 'Captain Fury' starring Brian Aherne (1902-1986) and Victor McLaglen (1886-1959). Unfortunately, soon after re-opening, both the organist and the new manager, Mr. J.J. Lambert, who had previously been with the New Ferry Lyceum, received their call-up papers for the war effort. Mrs. Crompton, the chief cashier, replaced the manager but no organist was provided.

Wallasey suffered badly during the German air-raids that commenced in May 1940 and one bomb narrowly missed the stage end of the Winter Gardens - demolishing the old dressing room block which had been part of the original theatre. However, the main cinema building escaped any serious damage.

The cinema again closed due to dwindling numbers because of the war at the beginning of 1941 and did not re-open until Whitsuntide, 1942. The opening attraction was Abbott and Costello film 'Hold That Ghost' with the famous BBC broadcasting and recording star Mr. Florence de Jong (1896-1990) entertaining on the organ. The organ was little used after this performance until November 1942 with the appointment of Charles Massey as both organist and manager.

Live shows were again introduced into the programme the following year. The most popular of these was Wednesday night talents spots which provided full houses. The popularity of these amateur shows led to 'Guest Night' stage shows on Friday evenings, when winners of the talent contests and some professional artists would be engaged. This continued even after Mr. Massey moved to open his own cinema, the Court, and was replaced by Mr. John Wright as organist and manager.

Stage shows had been dropped from the film programme by the early 1950's but there was a steep decline in audiences, as with all cinemas across Wallasey, which led to the owners, S.M Cinema, in 1954 renting the theatre to Nita Valaie and her Winter Garden Players who presented a summer season of plays from June until November. By the end of the year, S.M Group had sold the Winter Gardens to the Essoldo Circuit who installed Cinemascope before re-opening the cinema on 27th December 1954 with a showing of 'The Robe'. Essoldo staged their own stage shows from 21st May 1956 - 'Essoldo Follies' starring Eddie Malloy and Julie Dey plus Frank Gordon at the organ which had been moved into the orchestra pit. The final reversion to films occurred in October 1956, but in January 1957, the Winter Gardens closed with the double feature 'The Moonraker' staring Stanley Baker (1928-1976) and Sylvia Sims (1934-), plus John Ericson (1926-) in 'Oregon Passage'. This was the last of the New Brighton's four cinemas.

The building reopened in the mid 1960s as a Bingo Hall and was owned by Legalite Bingo but within a few years was bankrupt. The building was put up for auction with a reserve price of £15,000 but there were no takers. At one stage the building was sold to a firm of wood merchants for use as a warehouse but planning permission was not forthcoming. The building lay derelict for some years until being demolished to make way for new sheltered accommodation, called 'Winter Gardens' which was built on the site in 1992.

Trocadero Cinema

In 1919 a company was formed which acquired a block of shops as well as the Albert Billiard Hall in Victoria Road with the aim of converting the premises into a picture house. Mr. George Temperley was the managing director who had previously been the manager of the Liscard Palace in Seaview Road. The architects for the new building were Messrs. Wright and Hamlyn of Warrington and even though there were initial problems in gaining access to the billiard hall as well as a court battle to evict the original owners, the project was completed by the builders Messr. George Snape and Son of Birkenhead in 1922.

The Trocadero was built from reinforced concrete and was of fire-proof construction. The main frontage was executed in cream tinted terra cotta and the central portion, which rose above the

180

entrance, was finished with a heavy pedimented gable and well proportioned windows. Either side were lock-up shops surmounted by a plain parapet. Throughout the length of the frontage in Victoria Road, was a wrought-iron and glass veranda to provide shelter in bad weather for patrons queuing outside.

The cinema was capable of accommodating some 900 people inside in what was considered at that time, to be the most luxurious surroundings. The main entrance to the cinema had marble paving which provided access through mahogany swing doors that lead into a spacious hall panelled in keeping with the entrance doors. Leading directly from the hall were the entrance doors to the auditorium and immediately to the left was an elaborate staircase, with its massive balustrade. The stairs led to the foyer on the first floor, which in turn gave access to the luxurious balcony which had been constructed on a slope so as to ensure every seat had a clear view of the screen.

The inside walls were of simple and restrained style. The main piers were run up as plasterers finished with enriched brackets from which sprung arched ribs of decorative plasterwork across the ceiling. The intervening wall spaces between the plasterers were richly panelled in modelled plaster work leading up to an effective treatment over the circular windows, and surmounted at the eaves by a well-proportioned classic cornice. The infilling to the ceiling was also effectively broken up by a series of panels and enriched ventilating gratings. The proscenium front and arch was boldly treated forming a fitting frame to the silver screen and its drapers. The tip-up seats were upholstered in blue corduroy velveteen and finished with mahogany backs and arms. Heating the cinema was provided by a low-pressure hot water system, whilst the air conditioning comprised a blower fan to provide fresh, warm air at a low level to eliminate floor draughts.

The Trocadero was formally opened on 1st June, 1922 by the Mayor of Wallasey, Alderman Augustine Quinn. The first film shown was 'Perjury', staring William Farnum (1876-1953). A selection of comedies followed the film as well as news items and educational topics. Music was provided by the Tracadero Symphony Orchestra under the baton of Mr. Bescoby. The acting manager was Mr. C.H. Hankinson, who had previous experience with the Hippodrome and the Tivoli Theatre. The cost of admission was 6d, 9d and 1/3.

Even though the construction of the Trocadero had been financed by local businessmen, the cinema soon after opening changed hands to the Liverpool based First Federated Cinemas (J.F. Wood circuit). In 1928 it then became part of the rapidly expanding Gaumont-British circuit under whose control it remained until closure, the manager for many years being Robin Jones. The first talkie film to be shown was 'The Great Gabbo' with Erich von Stroheim (1885–1957) on Monday, 24th March, 1930.

The circle was reconstructed, re-seated and redecorated in November 1936 and the old alabaster light fittings being replaced by V-shaped metal framed pendant fittings, with amber tinted glass. The glass was removed from these fittings when war broke out in September 1939 to prevent the possibility of it being showered onto the audiences during the course of an air-raid. The fittings themselves were removed later on and replaced by a single large amber-coloured lamp in each instance.

The height of the screen at the cinema was a problem for front seat occupants because it was positioned on a very shallow stage platform, resulting in the first front rows having a distorted view of the image on the screen. In May 1944 Cinemascope was installed which gave a picture slightly wider than the original screen, but on 22nd September 1956, the Trocadero was closed with only a few days' warning. The cinema was converted into a supermarket for a time before being demolished.

New Brighton Court Cinema

Situated at 96/98 Victoria Road was New Brighton's first purpose-built cinema - Court Cinema. Opened on 6th December 1912, and compared to the standards of most cinemas, was a small, somewhat intimate theatre. It was described as "New Brighton's Cosy Picture Boudoir" with its best cinematic equipment and adequate ventilation to keep the air fresh and cool without creating draught. The internal decor was red and white with carpets, upholstery and light fittings setting the tone. The manager of the Court Cinema was Mr. Douglas Stuart.

The opening films, which included 'The Little Bear', 'Hydrogen', 'Henry VIII' and 'Romance at the Coat' were shown continuously from 7pm, with matinees on Mondays, Wednesday and Saturdays with admission at 3d, 5d and 1/-.

On Monday, 13th August 1931, "Perfect Talkies" was advertised, commencing with 'Near Rainbow's End' staring Bob Steele (1907-1988) and Louise Lorraine (1904-1981), and 'Borrowed Wives' with Rex Lease (1903-1966). Over the next couple of decades the cinema went through several changes in management, and in August 1940 when Mr. W.J. Speakman took control, much-needed new talkie apparatus was installed and some refurbishment took place. The Court re-opened in December 1943 and specialised as a New Theatre under the management of Charles Massey who had formerly managed the nearby Winter Gardens in Atherton Street. Two weeks later normal programmes of features films were re-instated as the venture was short lived.

After the Second World War the theatre was purchased by Whilma Wilkie, proprietor of the New Palace Amusement Park, who made

183

major modifications both internally and externally to the building. New Kalee projectors were on exhibition between 29th November and 4th December 1947 to the public in a nearby shop which was specially rented for the purpose. This equipment was in use from 8th December in the completely re-modelled and re-seated auditorium. For the first time as well, electrically-operated curtains were in use. A new canopy was provided for the exterior of the building.

It was not until 1955 that further changes took place with the installation of a wall-to-wall Cinemascope screen. This meant that seating accommodation had been reduced from 450 to 384. Due to lack of support and rising overheads the closure of the cinema in October 1958 was inevitable. The following year the Court re-opened in July with the emphasis on comedy films. The Court continued in business for another ten years before finally closing in March 1969 with William Holden's 'The Devil's Brigade'. In July 1988 Wirral magistrates made an order against George Wilkie and Co. ltd that the damp ridden building, which had been stripped of its interior and was just an empty shell, either be made safe or demolished within twenty-eight days. Soon afterwards the building was demolished.

Major Newspaper Articles

Tragedy at New Brighton

Liverpool Mercury Tuesday, 27th May, 1890

Felix Spicer, aged 60, described as a seaman, was yesterday brought before the magistrates at the Courthouse, Liscard, charged with the wilful murder of his son, William (aged 13 year old and two months) and Henry (aged 3 years and eight months), by cutting their throats at New Brighton on Sunday morning. He was further charged with having attempted to murder Mary his wife.27 The magistrates were Captain A.M Molyneux, Mr James Smith, and Mr W. Heap, and Colonel Hamersley, chief constable of Cheshire, occupied a seat on the bench. It being generally known that Spicer was to be brought up, there was a large attendance of the general public. After some ordinary trivial cases had been disposed of, Spicer was placed in the dock. He is a short, thick-set man, with scanty white hair, and full moustache beard and whiskers turning from sandy to grey. Throughout the proceedings, a policeman being by his side, he stood in the dock with his left hand on the rail, the fingers nervously and incessantly beating a tattoo, whilst his right hand hung lifelessly by his side. His aspect was that of a pre-occupied man, and only occasionally he betray a keen sense of interest in what was going on. The

27 Liverpool Mercury Tuesday, 27th May, 1890

magistrates' clerk read over the formal indictments, and when he came to the end of the first one, charging the prisoner with having "feloniously, and of malice aforethought, killed and murdered-one William Spice", the prisoner interrupted him, saying with emphasis, "I deny it, sir". The clerk went on with the reading without further interruption.

Superintendent Hindley stated the case. The prisoner, he said, had been in New Brighton something like 18 years, during which time he had known him as keeping refreshment rooms. Some short time ago he lived in Windsor Street but he was sold up, and then went to live at 18 Richmond Street. Since he had been in Richmond Street, his wife had had a refreshment room, a lock up place, near New Brighton Ferry, and there appeared to have been some dispute between them in consequences of her refusal to allow his name to be put over the door. After the dispute the wife slept at the refreshment room, the prisoner stopping at 18 Richmond Street. On Saturday night last he went to the refreshment room after it had closed, knocked at the door, and asked to be admitted. She refused him admittance and went to bed, but about three o'clock in the morning she was aroused by the smashing of the windows. She jumped up, and, seeing the prisoner, she slipped her skirts on and made a rush to get out through the broken window. The prisoner attempted to prevent her, slashing at her with a knife, and inflicting several severe wounds. She ultimately succeeded in getting into the street, and finding shelter in a neighbouring house. Her nose was cut nearly through, her throat was cut across, and her hands were badly wounded in trying to ward off the blows. She was now in the hospital, doing as well as could be expected. The police went to the house in Richmond Street, where they apprehended the prisoner, and they afterwards found that two of the children who slept there had been murdered in bed. A doctor was called, and he would state that, to the best of his knowledge, the children had been dead about three hours. It was only proposed to offer such evidence as would justify the bench in granting a remand for eight days. A woman named Fraser, who lived at 18 Richmond Street, would be called and would prove that the prisoner was in the house on Saturday night. It would also be proved that the prisoner's bed, was not occupied that night, and Mrs Fraser would tell the court that she heard the children screaming and the prisoner going about in the house. He thought this would satisfy their worships that his request for remand was a reasonable one.

Annie Fraser, wife of Archibald Fraser, 17 Greetham Street, Liverpool, was then called. She said she did not live with her husband, but had for some time been living with Mrs. Spicer as waitress, at 18 Richmond Street, New Brighton. Mrs. Spicer also kept a Refreshment Room at 3 Bickley Parade. Witness had been at the refreshment room on Saturday last, and left shortly after eleven o'clock at night to go to Richmond Street, where she slept. She arrived at the house about quarter to twelve, and saw the prisoner and the nurse girl, Mary, in the kitchen. The prisoner asked her where she had been, she replied that she had just come from the refreshment room. She saw he was in a very bad temper, so took no further notice of him, but said simply "Good night" and went upstairs to bed. She slept in a little room at the top of the stairs on the first landing, just opposite the front door. The nurse girl, who slept in the same room, went upstairs five minutes before her, and was undressing when she went up. Witness had commenced to undress when the prisoner called "Annie, I want you. Will you come and rub my shoulders?" She replied "Yes, certainly", and went downstairs and rubbed his shoulders. After which she bade him goodnight and went to bed. He bade her good night, and said he was going to sit up for the lodger, referring to a stranger who had engaged a bed at the refreshment room that day. Witness was suffering from indigestion, and passed a restless night, but was not disturbed by any noise. About break of day she got up and partly dressed herself and sat down on the side of the bed, and immediately after she sat down she heard the voice of the youngest deceased, Harry, cry out as though troubled in his sleep, and then a shuffling noise, as though his father, who had been in the habit of looking after the children since their mother had stayed away, was going to him. She could not say which room the person whose footsteps she heard went into. She afterwards lay down on the bed in her clothes and fell asleep, but had not slept long when she was awakened by the opening of the scullery back door, and heard some one, apparently with slippers on, run swiftly upstairs and down again, as though he had run up to fetch something. The person, whoever it was, was not upstairs as much as a minute. About three minutes or so after that she heard a loud knocking at the front door, and then some one outside her bedroom door said "we want you". She opened the door and saw Mr.Storey and Dr.Ross, Dr.Bride's assistant, coming upstairs, and one or two policemen in the lobby. She never saw the prisoner from the time she went to bed. Mrs.Spicer had not been in the house for a month or five weeks. Witness left her that night at the refreshment room. Mr.Spicer usually slept in the front bedroom. Witness went into that room on the Sunday morning and saw that the bed had not been used. Mr.Spicer was expecting a lodger, and the lodger had not turned up, and she did not think that Mr.Spicer had been to bed at all. He had told her that he was going to sleep on the sofa.

Supt Hindley --: Can you give the bench any ideas, from your own knowledge, why Mrs.Spicer did not go to 18 Richmond Street to sleep? Yes; when Spicer came home from sea he wanted to take possession, and Mrs.Spicer naturally objected. --: When did he come back from sea? In September I think, and Mrs. Spicer has kept him ever since. --: Was there any unpleasantness about this? Not then. He was right enough until last Easter. He and his wife were quite friendly until two or three days after Easter, when they had words about the refreshment room being put in Mr.Spicer's name, but they did not have a real quarrel until the following Monday. On that day Mrs.Spicer went to town, and whilst she was in town he took the money. When she returned she saw the money on the shelf where he had placed it, and she took it up and put it in her pocket. Mr.Spicer said, "leave that there" and she said "no, it doesn't require two to take money here." Then they had some words, and Mrs.Spicer asked witness quietly, without Mr.Spicer hearing, if she would go up to the house and send her bed down, saying she did not wish to go home with him. She sent a girl down with the bed, and Mrs.Spicer had slept at the refreshment room ever since. The bed was kept in the daytime in the kitchen under the dresser, and made up at night in the refreshment room. The slippers produced were Mrs.Spicer's

The prisoner, on being asked, if he wished to put any questions to the witness, replied quietly:

"No, sir".

Alfred Short, a clerk, was the next witness. He said he occupied a front room on the ground floor at 18 Richmond Street, as a sitting and bed room. On Saturday evening he went to bed at a quarter-past eleven o'clock, leaving the prisoner in the kitchen sitting on the sofa, and William, the elder of the two deceased children, sitting on a chair beside the sofa. Witness bade him good night and went to bed, leaving with him at his request, as he generally did, his watch, so that he might know the time in the morning. Witness soon went to sleep, but he was awakened shortly afterwards by a little alteration between Mr.Spicer and Mrs.Fraser. He heard Spicer speak very loudly to her about being late, but he did not hear her reply. He went to sleep again, and heard nothing more until he was awakened by two policemen coming into his bedroom in the morning. He got up and dressed himself, and heard Mr.Storey say - "he has murdered his two children". He went upstairs with Police-constable Potts (204), and, going into the

190

back bedroom where the children slept, saw them lying, one at the foot and the other at the head of the bed, with their throats cut. They were both dead, and there was a great quantity of blood about - in fact, the place was like a slaughter house.

F.Potts (P.C 204) stated that he was on duty in Rowson Street, New Brighton, about five minutes to four o'clock on Sunday morning in company with Police-constable A.Jones (301), when a young man came up to them, and, in consequence of information he gave them, they went to the refreshment room, Bickley-parade. Finding no one there they went to 18 Richmond Street, accompanied by Mr.Storey, whom they saw coming from the doctor's. Mr.Storey and he stayed at the front of the house whilst Constable Jones went to the back. Having obtained an entrance, Jones opened the front door and let them in. Jones arrested the prisoner, and Storey and witness went upstairs and found the two deceased boys in the back bedroom on the second landing. They were both dead. Witness remained there until the arrival of Dr.Rose and Police-sergeant Cooper. Mrs.Fraser gave him two letters (produced) in the lobby of the house about six o'clock that morning. One was in an envelope, unopened.

Sergeant Samuel George Cooper said he called at the police station, New Brighton, at 25 minutes past four o'clock on Sunday morning, and saw the prisoner there in custody of Police-constable 301, and from what the Constable said to him he went to 18 Richmond Street. On his return, about six o'clock, he examined the prisoner, and found blood stains on both his shirt wristbands and partly up the sleeves. There were also blood stains on the knee of his trousers and down each trouser leg - mostly on the right knee and leg - on the breast of his coat, and on the back and front of a pair of sand shoes which he was wearing.

The articles were produced, and caused a sickening sensation.

On the usual question -- "Have you anything to ask this witness"? being put to the prisoner, he replied -- "They are not bloodstains, sir, it is red paint on the shoes".

The Clerk to the Magistrates -- You will, of course, have an opportunity of speaking for yourself later.

The Prisoner -- Yes sir; very good.

The Chairman -- Your case will be remanded until the 2nd June at ten o'clock in the morning.

The Prisoner -- I would like to have a little assistance to defend me. I have no means at present.

The Clerk -- You get assistance on the trial.

The Prisoner -- I would like to have it now if I could get it. I could explain lots of things to you. There are some letters there which would explain the whole of it.

The Clerk -- You had better not say much now. Have you no money?

The Prisoner -- No

After a consultation with the clerk, the magistrates, through the chairman, said -- We have no power to meet you in any way at this stage.

The prisoner was then removed.

The Yorkshire Herald Wednesday, 28th May, 1890

An inquest on the victims of the New Brighton murder was opened yesterday. Mr. Caurton, coroner, commented on the conduct of Colonel Hamersley, Chief Constable, in removing the prisoner to Walton Gaol, and not allowing him to appear at the inquest. The Coroner said he will write to the Home Secretary. The Inquest was adjourned till to-morrow. It was stated that at the time the prisoner married Mrs. Spicer he had another living wife.28

Liverpool Mercury Thursday, 29th May, 1890

The funeral of the two victims of the murder at New Brighton on Sunday last, William and Henry Spicer, took place yesterday at Wallasey Cemetery, Rake Lane, Liscard. The interest naturally taken by the inhabitants of the district in the shocking event was the cause of a large assemblage of spectators at the house in Richmond Street and at the cemetery. Steps had been taken by a number of gentlemen, including Mr. Henry Spencer (the foreman of the coroner's jury). Mr. James Boughhey, Mr. John Bailey, and Mr. Berriman, to raise by public subscription to buy a grave in the cemetery, defray the expense of the burial, and temporarily maintain the remaining children.29 The funeral procession, consisting of a hearse and three mourning coaches. left the house about half- past three. The coffins were covered with wreaths and crosses sent by sympathising neighbours and friends, and each bore an inscription recording the names, date of death, and ages of the boys. The chief mourners were the sisters and brother of the deceased - namely Gertrude, Annie, Ethel, and Thomas Spicer. Mrs. Fraser, the waitress at Mrs. Spicer's refreshment room, occupied the one of the carriages with two of the children, and the attendance included most of the members of the coroner's jury and several New Brighton tradesmen. The burial service was conducted by the Rev. John H. Gwyther, pastor of the Congregational Church, Rice Lane, Liscard.

---

28 *The Yorkshire Herald Wednesday, 28th May, 1890*

29 Liverpool Mercury Thursday, 29th May, 1890

The Dundee Courier & Argus Friday, 30th May, 1890

Additional information was taken by the Cheshire Coroner yesterday in the case of the murder of two children by Felix Spicer, their father.30 Mrs. Spicer, who was terribly injured on the morning of the murder, said they were not married. He took her at sixteen under promise, and when the first child was born she pressed him to marry her, but he laughed at her in her shame and misery. A few days before the tragedy he told her landlord they were not married, and from that day she determined no longer to live with him, a declaration which brought about last Sunday's tragedy. The Inquest was again adjourned.

The North-Eastern Daily Gazette Thursday, 30th May, 1890

Yesterday at the adjourned inquest on the two children murdered by their father, Felix Spicer, at New Brighton, Cheshire, the mother, who was terribly injured, in her encounter with the accused, gave evidence. She said prisoner took her from home under the promise of marriage when she was 16. Though she pressed him to do so, he never married her. She had seven children by him. She kept him by means of the refreshment rooms. 31

He was of ungovernable temper, and had recently told her landlord that they were not married, which caused her to determine no longer to live with him. He then begged her forgiveness, whereupon she wrote the following to him "You told Mr. Wright I was not your wife, you mean, contemptible scoundrel. Did you think of my tears (her first child) I begged you to marry

---

30 The Dundee Courier & Argus Friday, 30th May, 1890

31 The North-Eastern Daily Gazette Thursday, 30th May, 1890

me out of my shame, and you laughed at me? But I have waited, and the day has come. I can tell everyone my tale, for I hated you since the day you laughed at me. I don't regard my name now. Why should I? Now everybody knows; but there is one thing I want you to know - the gallows before another night under the same roof as you. I will neither see you or be annoyed by you. You can remain in the house as long as you keep away from me. I will see the rent paid, but remember that I shall never change as long as I live". The woman was much affected whilst giving her evidence. The case was adjourned till next Wednesday.

Manchester Times Saturday, 31st May, 1890

A shocking tragedy was enacted early on Sunday morning at New Brighton. Mary Spicer carries on the business of a refreshment house keeper in Victoria Road, where she resides, and her husband resides in Richmond Street, the wife,32 it is said, having refused to live with him. On Saturday night Spicer assisted in putting his five children to bed, and between two and three o'clock on Sunday morning he cut the throats of two of them whilst they were in bed. Spicer then went to the Victoria Road house, where he attempted to murder his wife. She, though terribly cut about the arms and face, effected her escape by jumping through the bedroom window, her husband making a similar leap. The crash of glass brought the police to the spot, and they pursued the murderer and captured him in his house in Richmond Street. The police, on entering the house, found the sons, William and Henry. lying dead, with their throats cut from ear to ear. Jealousy is suppose to have been the cause of the tragedy. The house in Richmond Street is let to lodgers, all of whom were sound asleep when the police entered on

---

32 Manchester Times Saturday, 31st May, 1890

Sunday morning and apprised them of the murder of the two children.

Felix Spicer was brought before the Wallasey (Cheshire) magistrates on Monday and was remanded till Monday next.

At New Brighton Police Station on Tuesday morning, before Mr. C.W Tibbits. deputy-coroner, there was opened an inquiry into the cause of the death of William and Henry Spicer. The first witness called was Annie Fraser, who lived at the house where Spicer resided. She spoke of hearing Spicer walking about the house on the morning of the murder. Mrs. Spicer had lived with her husband at Richmond Street till the week after Easter Monday, when she went to 3, Bickley Parade, where she carried on business as a refreshment house keeper. There were six children, all of whom were living at Richmond Street, except the eldest, who was at Cardiff. Spicer himself had formerly been a ship's cook. Mr. and Mrs. Spicer were on comfortable terms till the week after Easter. At that, however, a quarrel took place, Mrs. Spicer saying her husband had no right to touch the money at the refreshment place, as she was mistress there. The next day Spicer said he would show her who is master, but he did not offer to assault her in any way. He was a very passionate man. She saw Spicer on Saturday evening when she went up to Richmond Street for something. He then told her to ask Mrs. Spicer if he might go down to the rooms that week, and she sent word back that she did not want him for that week, nor did she ever want to set eyes on him again. On Saturday night witness got into the house at a quarter to twelve, when she found Spicer sitting in the kitchen. He was perfectly sober, but was in a bad temper. About daylight, feeling restless, she got up and sat by the window. The two deceased children slept in the room adjoining witness's, and Spicer slept in a room by himself. While witness was awake she heard someone go into the children's room, but did not pay much attention to the circumstances, as Mr. Spicer had been in the habit lately of looking after the children. Afterwards there was a loud knocking at the front door. Some persons were let into the house, and she was told the children were murdered. Police constable 204 (Potts) deposed that he received information of the murder of the children. At the time prisoner was arrested it was not known that the children were murdered. He was taken into custody on suspicion of having wounded his wife. He was very cool, was sober, and did not offer any resistance. He said to Jones, "I have done nothing". -- Mr. Churton, the coroner, who had entered the court in the course of the inquiry, asked : "Is the prisoner here"? -- Sergeant Cooper : "No". -- Mr Churton : "Why not"? -- Sergeant Cooper : "He has been sent to Walton". -- Mr Churton : "For the last forty years I have never held an inquest without having the prisoner present, and for the simple reason that he is afforded an opportunity before the coroner of making a statement which he cannot do before the magistrates. His mouth is closed there. It is a strange thing that he should be sent away. I shall take certain steps myself this evening in regard to this matter". -- Dr. F.W.F Ross stated that he was called about 4.15 on Sunday morning, and went down to 18 Richmond Street, where he found the children William and Henry lying on a bed. They were dead, and the wounds which had caused their deaths must have inflicted by a very sharp instrument. -- In reply to the Coroner, a policeman stated that no instrument had been found. -- The inquest was afterwards adjourned.

With regard to Mrs. Spicer, it may be stated that though terribly injured by the knife with which her husband attacked her, the injuries are not likely to lead to fatal results, and it is expected by next Monday she will be able to give evidence.

The Dundee Courier & Argus Monday, 2nd June, 1890

Interview with the Prisoner:

On Saturday. Alfred Short, who lodged in the house of Felix Spicer, the man charged with murdering his children at New Brighton, had an interview with Spicer in Walton Gaol. When asked about the crime, prisoner said, "I know nothing about it, so help me God. I washed little Harry, and kissed him and put him to bed, and bade him good night, bless his little heart". Here the prisoner wept bitterly. "Willie", he continued amid his sobs, "went to bed about about half-past eleven.33 I wished him good night, and know no more of either of them. I am as innocent as you are". Again his sobs interrupted his statement and when he became calm he continued -- "I am remained in the kitchen until three o'clock in the morning, when I went down to the refreshment rooms of my wife. The knife I used to the woman was my clasp knife, which was taken possession of by the police. In further conversation, the prisoner said he would not tell a lie to hurt any soul breathing. He referred to his love for the children, and said the woman had brought it all upon herself by refusing to forgive him. At parting he he told his visitor to tell his wife that he forgave her. He sent his love to her, although she had been very cruel to him.

The Sheffield & Rotherham Independent Monday, 2nd June, 1890

On Saturday morning the police renewed the search for the knife used by Spicer in the murder of his two children and the attack on

---

33 The Dundee Courier & Argus Monday, 2nd June, 1890

his wife last Saturday.34 After pulling up the flooring of the various rooms, search was made in about a cooking stove, when the knife was found in one of the flues. It bore ample evidence of the crime. The police have also ascertained the whereabouts of the missing lodger., who will be called at the adjourned inquest next Wednesday.

Liverpool Mercury Tuesday, 3rd June, 1890

Accused before The Magistrates

The Bench & Newspaper Comment

At the Liscard Courthouse, yesterday, Felix Spicer, a ship's rigger, aged 60 years old, was charged on remand with the murder of his sons William and Henry Spicer, aged 14 and 4 years respectively, and also with having attempted to murder Mary Palin, at New Brighton, on May 25. The magistrates present were Captain Molyneux (presiding), Messrs James Smith, W.Heap, and W.B Marshall. Mr. R.B Moore defended the accused. Colonel Hamersley, chief constable of Cheshire, was also present, and Superintendent Hindley, assisted by Sergeant Cooper, had charge of the case on behalf of the police. The trial was fixed to commence at ten o'clock, and although the courthouse is situated away from a busy thoroughfare, there was a large crowd outside. The public were admitted to the back part of the court, and a fierce struggle ensued on the part of the crowd which endeavored to squeeze itself into a "gallery" capable of accommodating only one hundred persons. Spicer, who had been in weak health in the last few days, was brought from Walton Jail and driven in a cab to the court. He

---

34 The Sheffield & Rotherham Independent Monday, 2nd June, 1890

looked careworn, but seemed to follow the proceedings with an intelligent interest, keeping his eyes fixed on the witnesses, and occasionally be consulted with his solicitor. Owing to some remarks in an interview published in a Liverpool paper, the chairman made a statement hoping that such statements would not again be published. Mrs. Spicer, who was accompanied into court by her sister, a resident of Cardiff, gave a clear account of the terrible struggle she had had with the accused, and two witnesses who had watched the affair from their windows supplemented her testimony. The lady, who wore a dark ulster and veil, was deeply affected, and when the question was put to her,35 "have you been to 18 Richmond Street since", she replied "no", and then burst into tears. Her wrists were still covered with bandages, and as she leaned on the solicitors table, at which she was seated while giving her evidence, a plain gold band was observable on the third finger of her left hand. Her depositions having been read over to her, she signed her name "Mary Palin". The bench then remanded the accused until Monday next, and refused a request made by Mr. Moore that for convenience in consulting for the defence the prisoner might remain in Liscard, and not be removed to Walton. A number of persons remained outside the court house until after five o'clock, when the court adjourned, and witnessed the departure the cab which conveyed Spicer back to Walton Jail.

Maria Fearon, aged 15 years, stated that she was the nurse-girl employed by Mrs. Spicer. She repeated her evidence as to putting the children to bed on the night of May 24. After going down to the refreshment rooms witness returned to Richmond Street and gave the prisoner his supper, but he said he could not eat any. Witness went to bed about twelve o'clock, and soon after Mrs. Fraser, who had had some words with Fearon, also went to bed. By

---

35 Liverpool Mercury Tuesday, 3rd June, 1890

Superintendent Hindley : She heard no arrangement made as to which beds the children were to occupy. While Spicer was in the kitchen a man came in, and Spicer said, "I'm very sorry, old pal, I have no room for you to-night;" at the time returning the man's umbrella. The man went out with Spicer, and she did not see him again. She had not seen him before. Spicer had told her that four lodgers coming that night.

Mr. Moore, at the close of the witness's examination-in-chief, said that as he understood the examination of the various witnesses would not finish that day he proposed to adjourn his cross-examination. It was most desirable that after hearing the evidence he should have an interview with the accused, and go through the evidence line by line. He had had an interview with the prisoner that morning, and received an outline from him, and it was a very long business.

James Thomas Lea, architect and surveyor, produced plans of the house 18 Richmond Street, New Brighton, and refreshment room, 3, Bickley Parade, and the surrounding streets. The distance between the two places was 325 yards.

Dr. Frederick William Forbes Ross, in partnership with Dr. Bride, and practising at Victoria Road, New Brighton, gave evidence similar to that given at the coroner's inquiry with reference to the position and conditions of the bodies of the children found at 18 Richmond Street after the murder. He said the knife shown to him by Sergeant Cooper, on Saturday, might probably have caused the wounds on the bodies. They were caused by a cutting instrument. The knife shown to him was a short one, with a brown wooden handle, and a blade nearly four inches long, and there were blood stains and soot on it. When he arrived at the house the children had been dead for about an hour. By Superintendent Hindley : Subsequently, he saw the prisoners clothing. The shirt had blood stains on the cuffs, and there were a few spots scattered across the

201

breast and body. He saw the shirt on Spicer within half an hour after he had examined the scene of the murder, and it was decided that it should be taken off him. He did not examine the shirt sufficiently to say whether the blood spots were on the front of the shirt. He went to the prisoner, and asked to look at hands. He told Spicer he had washed them, and the reply was, "Indeed sir, I have not washed them this morning." Witness then said, "you lie, Spicer" and asked the officer to turn up his cuffs. The policeman did so, and witness found that both wrists and a portion of the arm were smeared with blood, and there was a waterline showing where the washing process had stopped.

Superintendent Hindley -- Did you notice any cuts on his hands?
Witness -- There were no new cuts which could have caused this blood.
The Superintendent -- Could this blood have got on the shirt if he had had his coat on?
Witness -- Possibly, but I do not think it could have got on the body of the shirt.
The Superintendent -- Did you notice blood anywhere else?
Witness -- Yes, on the latch of the back gate of 18 Richmond Street, on the kitchen floor, and also on the inside of the handle of the scullery door.

I looked for blood outside, but did not find any. The bloodstains found on the handle need not have been visible to the eye; they might have been left there by a clumsily-washed hand. He tested for the stains chemically. He applied the same tests to the prisoner's clothes, which were handed to him by Sergeant Cooper, and found fresh bloodstains on all the garments. Some of the stains on the shirt were quite fresh. At the same time the sergeant showed him a piece of wood which had been sawn to leave a sort of handle, and on this was blood, half dried. A bloody hand had grasped the handle so that the blood had gone into the wood. This piece of wood was lying on the pavement in front of the window the prisoner was said to have smashed. He found this wood about 20 minutes after he had left the children. He had seen the wife just before this, and found her in a state of shock, pale and exhausted, at Mr. Bailey's. She was slashed across the bridge of the nose, but the hemorrhage was ceasing. There was a wound on her right-hand palm, and one on the left forearm.

The Superintendent -- Would the amount of blood the wife lost be sufficient to account for the amount of blood on the prisoner's clothes?

Witness -- I don't think so. I do not think it would account for the blood on the right knee of the prisoner's trousers. I had found stains on the head of the bed, showing that there had been blood smeared by a knee in three places. On examining the prisoner's trousers at the police station I found there was a stain on them just below the right knee. It was quite moist, and had soaked through, and had soaked through the cloth, marking the prisoner's knee.

John Bailey, grocer, 4 Victoria Road, New Brighton, stated that about 20 minutes to four o'clock on the morning of the May 25 he was awakened by his wife, who told him she heard someone screaming. He got out of bed, and went to the window, which overlooked Victoria Road. He saw Mr. and Mrs. Spicer, whom he knew by sight, on the parapet in front of Bickley Parade. They were struggling together. He was kneeling with both knees on the lower part of her body. With the left hand he seemed to grasp the hair of her head, and with the right hand he was working away across her throat. He saw the prisoner's closed hand go up and down each time, and it seem to have been arrested by Mrs. Spicer each time he seemed to strike. He could not say whether the prisoner had a knife or anything in his hand. Witness raised an alarm by shouting "murder", "police", and blew a whistle. This had no effect, so he called to Spicer by name, saying "Spicer, this is too abusive". He received no answer, and Spicer did not look up, but continued in the same position. Witness left the window, and put on some clothing, and went out into the road. Spicer and his wife were on their legs, the latter standing at the back the cabmen's shelter, and having her back towards the river. The prisoner was on the north-east angle of the shelter, nearer to No. 3 Bickley Parade. Seeing the prisoner make an attempt to run after her the witness called to him "Spicer don't do that; you must not do any more". Witness called to Mrs. Spicer to run into the house as the door was open. She hesitated for a moment, and then started. She went into the house, and witness followed and closed the door. He did not see the prisoner again. She was bleeding dreadfully from various parts of the face and arm - in fact, she was a ghastly sight. He did not see a knife of any sort in the prisoner's hand.

Francis Storey was the next witness called, but before he commenced the magistrates left the bench for a few minutes, and on returning to the court :
The Chairman said : The attention of the bench has been called to some remarks in one of the Liverpool newspapers of this date. They wish to say that they think in the interests of justice some of the remarks should not have been made, and they hope that nothing of this kind will be said again. At the same time, they wish the witness to know that they have nothing to be afraid of if they tell the truth; and if any threats are made to them they should communicate at once with the police, who will see that they are protected.
Mr. Moore -- I am unaware of any threats having being used, directly or indirectly, either by my client or myself or my friends. The hearing of the evidence was then resumed.

Mr. Storey said he was a general dealer, at 3 Victoria Road. On May 25 about quarter to four o'clock in the morning, he was awakened by hearing screams and a cry of "murder", "police". He

204

got up and went to the bedroom window, and saw a man and a woman struggling on the parade. While putting on some clothes, with the intention of going down, he heard more shouting from next door, and on going to the window again he saw the woman running up the road with the man after her. As he passed under the window witness saw a short knife blade in his hand. Witness had the impression that the knife was rounded off at the top. The man caught up to the woman outside Bailey's window and grasped her about the shoulders. He had the knife in his hand raised. Witness saw no more as he hurried from the window to get dressed as he considered the matter had become very serious. Mrs. Storey soon after told him the woman had got into Bailey's and was safe, so he did not hurry downstairs, but on again looking through the window he saw the prisoner, whom he then recognised, go to Mrs. Spicer's house and smash the window with a plank of wood. Having committed the damage he put the piece of wood down by the side of the parapet and then entered the refreshment rooms through one of the broken windows. Witness came downstairs and went into Mr. Bailey's house, where he saw Mrs. Spicer, and on coming out he informed the police as to the direction in which Spicer had gone. He afterwards accompanied the police to 18 Richmond Street, and while they were in the parlour the prisoner walked from the kitchen, and was arrested by Police constable Jones. When they got outside the house witness told Constable Potts he had better go and see if the children were all right, and he did so. Sergeant Cooper afterwards showed witness blood stains on the frame on the window at Bickley Parade, through which the prisoner had entered. There was a pool of blood where the struggle had taken place.

Gertrude Annie Spicer, aged eight years, living at 18 Richmond Street, repeated the evidence she had given before the coroner, the principal point being that during the night on which the murder was committed she heard her brother cry. She called out "what's the matter, Harry"? and someone whom she thought was her father, replied "Go to sleep".

Mrs. Spicer was then called, and it was with great difficulty that she could compose herself to give her evidence. She said her name was Mary Palin. She had known the prisoner for 17 years. She was 32 years of age, and lived with him at 18 Richmond Street. The had had seven children. The prisoner came back in September after a nine month's voyage. He had not been to sea for 15 years prior to that. She slept at 18 Richmond Street until the week following Easter, when she commenced to stay at the refreshment rooms. She did this because of something the prisoner had told Mr. Wright. The witness repeated the evidence given before as to the dispute Spicer and she had on Monday after Easter with regard to the money received at the refreshment rooms. She told him he had nothing to do with business, and this seemed to annoy him very much. He said he would let her see whether he had nothing to do with it. He pulled off his coat and knocked about the things in the place, and she called in Police sergeant Whitchurst, to whom she showed her tenant's agreement. The sergeant told him she had the power to put him out, and after that he became very quiet. She then had a bed brought down to the refreshment rooms. She did so not because she was afraid, but because she thought it might save a quarrel. She had not intended to stay more than the night, but she decided to stay longer because of the prisoner going to the landlord. After this, Spicer sent messages and notes asking her to come back and begging her pardon.

Letters written by the prisoner to the witness were then put in. In the first one read the prisoner addressed her "my dear Polly", and asked that "by the great God forgive me, and do not always cast me out with a broken heart. Do forgive me. Have mercy on me, and I will make every amend in my power. Have mercy on me, have mercy on me. As a good girl give me some proof of your

206

friendship. Yours for ever, F. SPICER". On the back of this sheet in the handwriting of Mrs. Spicer was the reply - "You are too late, and you need not to try to see me. The door is locked, and once for all I will not be annoyed by you. I shall not see you". A letter written by Spicer on May 19 last, and the reply from the witness (which have been published), were next read, as also a letter written by the prisoner to Mr. A. Wright saying that it was a great trial to him, as, being the founder of the business, that more favourable consideration had not been shown to him. He added that he was afraid Mr. Wright had been misinformed about his affairs, and he asked for Mr. Wright to reconsider his decision so that he can work in the rooms in amicable way, which he gave his honest word should be peace and love. He closed by saying "I am, now broken-heartened." The next letter put in was addressed to the witness and was as follows :- "I will call down tonight about nine o'clock. I hope you will consider my feelings and forgive me, and make it up and shake hands. I am a broken man. For God's sake and have pity on me. - Yours for ever - F.SPICER".

The witness, continuing, said she believed he came down on the night after the letter was written. They had a conversation, and she refused to make the quarrel up. On the night May 24 the prisoner came to the refreshment rooms about half-past ten o'clock just as she was locking up. He knocked at the door, and she asked who was there. He called out to her to open the door, but she replied that she could not as she was undressing. He bade her good night, and she returned the wish. He then repeated "Good night girl" and walked away. In the afternoon of that day she made an arrangement with a gentleman who wanted lodgings, and referred him to 18 Richmond Street. Before she went to bed the girl Fearon came down to the refreshment room and returned to Richmond Street. This would be about half past eleven o'clock. The witness described the attack on her as follows : Early the next morning, when it was quite daylight, I was awoke by the crash of glass. I jumped out of bed and saw Spicer through the window. He had his arm through the side window feeling for the key of the door inside. I put on some clothes and my slippers. When Spicer found there was no key he broke another window. I jumped up on to the partition and tried to get through the window, and in doing so overbalanced him on the other side. He leaped on to me and held me down. He had a white handkerchief or piece of linen in his hand, and it spelled of brandy or some kind of spirits. He was trying to get it on my face. I got it out of his hand. He had nothing else in his hands. I saw him try to get something out of his right breast pocket, and I thought it was a revolver. I saw it was something brown. I had screamed murder when I first jumped out of the window, and he kept saying "you scream murder, you scream murder, but you won't scream murder, you - wretch, in a minute, when I have done with you". By this time I saw it was a knife he had got out of his pocket. It was not a clasp knife. I had seen the knife before, and it has been shown to me by Sergeant Cooper. Spicer struggled for some time, and I held on to his coat sleeve and kept guarding off the knife. He aimed all the time at my throat, and I drew my skirt around my neck with the left hand, using the right hand to ward off the knife. I was obliged to hold on to the blade for some time, and I kept asking him to spare me for God's sake and for the sake of the children. My right hand was cut through holding on to the knife. My left hand was injured with the glass.

I could not tell when my face was cut; I found afterwards that I was cut and bleeding.
Mr Solly -- How did you get away from him?
Witness – I can hardly say. I knocked the knife out of his hand, and that gave me the opportunity for escaping. I looked around and saw the neighbours in the window. I ran up past Mr. Bailey's, and

then came back and got on one side of the cabmen's hut, and Spicer was on the other side. I was dodging him round the hut. Mr. Bailey came to his door and called me to his house, where I entered. Spicer had walked away towards Bickley Parade. The cut on my nose was done by Spicer, I think, when I was escaping. After I knocked the knife out of hand he stooped to pick it up, and then it was I managed to escape.

By Superintendent Hindley -- I had heard nothing about four lodgers coming to Richmond Street before prisoner called at the refreshment rooms. I cannot say how the prisoner was dressed. He certainly had on a coat of some description, and was not in his short sleeves. He wore a cap, and the coat was a long one, I think. I had heard Mr. Bailey call to the prisoner, who turned round and, using foul language, told him to go in. I remember the prisoner on coming home, after his discharge from the Claremont, producing the knife, and saying it only cost 4d., but that it was worth half a-crown, and it would cut all the throats of New Brighton. I am not certain he said "cut the throats", it might have been "would settle all in New Brighton". This occurred before Christmas. He kept the knife in a box used for odds and ends.

Mr. Bailey, recalled, said that when he saw the prisoner on the Sunday morning he wore a kind of short overcoat. He had a peaked cap on his head, and slippers on his feet.

Mr. Storey, recalled, said the prisoner wore a blue coat and a 'cheese-cutter' cap.

The Bench decided to remand the accused until Monday next.

Mr. Moore said the date would suit him. There was a good deal to be done in the way of seeing the prisoner, and he asked the bench not to send the prisoner to Walton, but to retain him on the court premises.

209

The Chairman -- We have decided to remand the prisoner to Walton. They have every accommodation there for you to have consultations.

Liverpool Mercury Thursday, 5th June, 1890

The fund which was started for the benefit of Mrs. Spicer and her children some few days ago is still open and Mr. John Bailey, Victoria Road, is the honorary treasurer.36 Part of the money which has been received has been used to defray the expenses connected with the funeral of the children. Mrs. Spicer has expressed her gratitude for the kindly interest that has been taken in her.

Liverpool Mercury Tuesday, 10 June, 1890

Committal of "The Accused"

Yesterday, at the Wallasey Police Court, Felix Spicer was brought up on remand charged with having murdered his two sons, William and Henry Spicer, and also with having attempted to murder Mary Anne Palin, at New Brighton, on the morning of Whit Sunday, the 25th of May.

Mr A.T Wright, a member of the firm of Messrs. Wright, Becket & Co., solicitors, Liverpool, under whom the tenancy of the premises Bickley Parade was held. He said that on the 2nd May the prisoner called at his office and asked that he might have the tenancy of the premises, 3 Bickley Parade, which were at one time let to Mrs. Spicer. The prisoner had been a tenant of the shop until about Christmas 1888, and at that time had asked to have the premises taken off his hands, and as he could not pay all the rent he

---

36 Liverpool Mercury Thursday, 5th June, 1890

authorised witness to take the fixtures for the amount due. Spicer, at his last interview with witness, about Easter, urged that he should be allowed to resume the tenancy.37 He mentioned that Mrs. Spicer was not his wife, but displayed no ill-feeling against her. Witness told him that he was quite satisfied with Mrs. Spicer's tenancy, but if it was more satisfactory to him he would tell Mrs. Spicer to call at the office. Witness wrote to Mrs. Spicer, who called on the following Monday, and the result of the interview, together with other inquiries, was that witness wrote to the prisoner stating that he had heard Mrs. Spicer's story, and did not propose to make any change to the tenancy. He advised Spicer to seek employment elsewhere, and not to interfere in the business in any way.

Walter Edward Banning, a lamplighter [said] on Whit Sunday morning, about 2.15, he had heard the crying of the baby at the house in Richmond Street. On going to the front door he heard a light shuffle, as of feet, in the lobby, and that he heard a voice, but did not hear what was said. He again heard the child's voice, but, thinking it was a baby crying, went away.

Mrs. Fraser, the witness at the refreshment room, was recalled, and repeated a portion of her evidence, already published. In cross examination by Superintendent Hindley, witness said that about a week or a fortnight before the murder the prisoner asked her how she got into the refreshment rooms in the mornings - if she had a key. She replied that Mrs. Spicer let her in, and that she had no key.

Joel Fitton, iron turner, 82, Wild Street, Derby, said that on the night of the murder he was staying at 5 Victoria Road, New Brighton, which is nearly opposite 3 Bickley Parade. About half

---

37 Liverpool Mercury Tuesday, 10 June, 1890

past three in the morning he was awakened by his boys knocking at his door. In consequence of what they said he ran downstairs to the sitting room window. From there he saw the prisoner and Mrs. Spicer struggling. Witness noticed a knife on the floor, which Spicer was trying to reach. Mrs. Spicer got away and went across the road to Mr. Bailey's and Spicer went towards the rooms. The knife witness saw on the floor looked something like a shoemaker's knife, and would be four or five inches long. He could not swear that the knife produced was the one he saw, but the knife had a dark handle. After the struggle Spicer went inside the refreshment room through the front window and witness heard the sound of running water, which gave him the impression that the prisoner was washing his hands. He then came out and went towards the shore, and turned along the lower parade.

Mary Ann Palin, known as Mrs. Spicer was recalled [and] was shown the knife produced by the analyst, which she recognised as the one with which the prisoner had attacked her on the night of the murder.

Charlotte Myers, wife of John Myers, 6 Richmond Street, New Brighton, said she kept a lodging house. On the night of the murder she saw the prisoner in Richmond Street about 20 minutes to eleven. After some conversation, the prisoner told her that his house was full of lodgers, and asked her to accommodate anyone who might turn up. She went home, and about eleven 'o clock Spicer, accompanied by a gentleman, called, and Spicer told her that he had brought a gentleman for the night. The lodger stayed in the house all night, and got up about seven o'clock. He paid for his bed, and left without having breakfast. She had not seen him since, and did not know his name. -- By Superintendent Hindley : She would of known if anyone had left the house during the night because she had put second lock on the door, and it could not have be shut from the outside.

212

Thomas Frederick Cooke, a plumber, 3 Belmont Road, New Brighton, stated that on the 31st May, he was assisting to search the premises of 3 Bickley Parade. In the cooking range, between the upper plate and the oven flue, he found the knife produced, and handed it to Constable Jones. The knife must of been put there through the manhole.

In relation to Alfred Short interview with Mr F. Spicer at Walton Jail, see Monday 2nd June: Sheffield & Rotherham News article.

Mr Moore to Mr. Short : This interview occurred on the 31st May at Walton Jail?

Witness : It did sir

Mr Moore : Was there any warders present?

Witness : There was one warder present, head warder, present.

Mr Moore : Had you an order from the Prison Commissioners to see the prisoner?

Witness : No sir.

Mr. Moore : Had you on the 26th May, been examined and given evidence along with other witnesses?

Witness : I had sir

By the Bench : My interview took place in consequence of a letter received from the prisoner. I had not previously written to him.

This concluded the evidence, and the formula of charging the prisoner was then gone through. In reply to the magisterial caution on the first charge, that of the murder of William Spicer, the prisoner, acting on the advice of his solicitor, replied that he was not guilty, and that he did not want to call any witnesses. He made the same reply to the second charge, that of the murder of Henry Spicer, adding that he would reserve his defence. In reply to attempting to murder Mary Ann Palin, he said he was guilty of the assault on her. He was then committed to the assizes at Chester on three charges.

Manchester Times Saturday, 14th June, 1890

The inquest on the victims of the New Brighton murder was resumed at Seacombe on Wednesday. The Coroner, in his address to the jury, again complained strongly of the action of the Home Secretary in refusing the prisoner to be brought into the Coroner's Court. The jury, after a short deliberation, returned a verdict to the effect that had been wilfully murdered by their father. Felix Spicer, now in custody in Knutsford Gaol.38

Some Popular Newspaper Reports

Liverpool Mercury, Friday 8th September, 1871

To The Editors Of The Liverpool Mercury.

Gentlemen, - in reference to a police report in today's Mercury *of a case of gross imposition on the part of donkey and horse drivers at New Brighton, will you permit me, as a resident of that district, to say a few words? The bad language these people use, their rapacity, and the quarrelsome deposition that characterises them, often bring them into strong collision with the excursionists, and scenes are enacted that more resemble the events at Donnybrook fair than those of a peaceful watering hole - save that there is no fighting, as at Donnybrook, for "love and good humour", In some respect the horses and donkeys are an unmitigated nuisance. The great advantage of living in such a locality as Wallasey is that it has a splendid shore, where, under ordinary circumstances,*

---

38 Manchester Times Saturday, 14th June, 1890

families might really enjoy the healthy and bracing air for which it is famous.39 But the truth is, these donkeys and horses, goaded and tormented by their drivers, and doubly so by the majority of the persons who mount them, who know no more how ride on horseback than they know how box the compass, go rushing about the shore in the most reckless manner, so that persons walking have constantly to exercise all their skill to avoid being run over. As for ladies and children, they are excluded in this way from the enjoyment the sands would otherwise afford, and, of course, the locality suffers to a corresponding extent. Where proper order is kept, as at other watering places, I have nothing to say against the harmless trotter of donkeys; but the wild galloping among the people which is daily permitted at New Brighton is not creditable to the local authorities -

Yours etc.

C.

Sept.5, 1871.

Liverpool Mercury, Saturday 2nd July, 1892

Tragedy at New Brighton

Great sensation was caused at New Brighton on Thursday by the discovery on the beach of the bodies of a woman and child, lying about high water mark. The discovery was made by two working men named Young and Bennett, who in passing along the shore at about six o'clock in the morning saw the remains at a spot beyond the Red Noses and to the north of the vessel known as "Noah's

---

39 Liverpool Mercury, Friday 8th September, 1871

215

Ark". They were lying on a grey striped macintosh.40 The woman appeared to be about twenty-eight years of age, and the child, a boy about twelve months old, was lying across her breast. The woman was well clad in a maroon coloured dress, blue bodice. two flannel singlets, new chemise marked W. (or M.) Robinson, and black stockings. She had a morocco purse, which contained a return ticket from Liverpool to Southport, issued on Saturday last, a pawnticket for three rings issued on Wednesday by Mr. Mason, Liverpool, who lent 3s. upon the articles. On the woman's body was found a letter scribbled in pencil on a rough sheet of paper. It ran :- "This is mother and son. Home and friends all gone; nothing to live for. We have friends at this address, Greenhithe, Huddersfield. Whoever finds us let them know. Robinson." The bodies were conveyed to the deadhouse at the Magazines, awaiting identification. The infant, from the way in which it was lying when discovered, must have been actually drawing from its mother's breast at the time of death. The unfortunate woman is entirely unknown either in New Brighton or the neighbourhood. There is little doubt that the deceased crossed over from Liverpool to New Brighton some time during Wednesday. The police have communicated with the authorities at Huddersfield, with a view of finding either relatives or friends; also with the Coroner (Mr. H. Churton), who held the inquest yesterday (Friday).

Liverpool Mercury, Thursday 11th April, 1895

The "Noah's Ark" Refreshment Rooms

William Hayes, 35 Pleasant Street, Liscard, was summoned [before Wallasey Police Court] for permitting a nuisance to exist at "Noah's Ark" refreshment rooms on the New Brighton shore. Mr. Pugh appeared for the Wallasey District Council, and Mr.

---

40 Liverpool Mercury, Saturday 2nd July, 1892

McConchie defended. A number of witnesses were called by. Mr. Pugh to show that a very foul smell proceeded from the interior of the "Ark", a vessel which had been stranded on the beach, and which is used as a refreshment room. In addition to the smells from the interior of the vessel there were also bad odours arising from the pools surrounding it. -- Mr. McConchie, for the defence, called witnesses, who stated that the smells from the vessel were no worse than those which arose from the decayed shell fish, &c., on other parts of the shore. He contended that the "Ark" was not "premises" under the Act, and did not come under the section. -- The Chairman said the bench had decided that the "Ark" was used as refreshment premises, and were also a nuisance. He thought the owner and the district council might come to terms. -- Mr. Danger : (law clerk to the council) said the defendant or his predecessors had brought the "Ark" there and ought to take it away. The negotiations to take it away had not been successful because the sum asked (£50) was considered too high. -- Mr. McConchie said that if the place was "premises" it was curious that the council had never rated them; and Mr Pugh in reply, pointed out that the council had control over the foreshore. -- Ultimately the Bench made an order that the "Ark" be removed within a period of two months.41

Liverpool Mercury, Thursday 4th July, 1895

The "Noah's Ark" Nuisance

William Hayes, 35 Pleasant Street, Liscard, was summoned [before Wallasey Police Court] for neglecting to carry out the order of the magistrates to remove the hulk called the Noah's Ark,

---

41 Liverpool Mercury, Thursday 11th April, 1895

lying on the shore at New Brighton.42 Mr. Bascombe, nuisance inspector, said nothing had been done since the case was last before the bench, except that a piece of the stern had been removed. The nuisance was now almost as bad as when the case was first brought up in April. Mr. W. Danger, clerk to the district council, said that a fortnight ago the bench imposed a nominal continuous penalty. The defendant said he had offered the wreck to the district council, and he could do no more. He had no means of removing it. Mr. Danger said the council would be willing to take the wreck and get rid of it, but for there being several owners. A little gunpowder would blow it up. The Chairman said the bench were proceeding by stages, and would continue to do so. Defendant would be fined 5s. per day for the 14 days covered by the summons, and 8s. 6d. costs -- £3. 18s. 6d. in all.

New Brighton - Skeleton Found

Liverpool Mercury, Tuesday 19th September, 1876

TO CORRESPONDENTS

"On Tuesday last the workers engaged excavating for the foundation of the New Brighton Aquarium found the skeleton of a human body, which they placed in a shed on the ground.43 The remains were found about three feet below the flooring of one of the houses that originally stood there, known by the name of the "Devil's Nest", and which were pulled down two years ago. Up to this day (Monday) the skeleton still remains in the shed, and, though known to the police, no action has been taken; and my object in writing you is in hope that an inquiry might be held, and

---

42 Liverpool Mercury, Thursday 4th July, 1895

43 Liverpool Mercury, Tuesday 19th September, 1876

so put an end to the indifferent rumour now in circulation, for about 18 years ago a builder from Seacombe, after leaving here for his home, was never afterwards seen."

Watch.
New Brighton.

Popularity

The Popular Seaside Resort

NEW BRIGHTON TOWER

The popularity of New Brighton - the principal Seaside Resort in the County of Cheshire - increases daily, and deservedly so, for not only can health, pleasure and amusement be found there, but situated as it is at the estuary of the noble River Mersey as it enters the Irish Sea, it offers the visitor a glorious view of Liverpool's Great Waterway and the finest Panorama of Shopping in the world. No other seaside resort possesses so many natural advantages as the famous Cheshire resort. It offers an education, real and lasting, and as the leviathans of the shipping world pass by, one gains an impression of England's greatness which can never be effaced from the mind. It is a slight and an instruction that is without parallel and one can readily understand why this beautiful resort is the most favoured among excursionists from all parts of Lancashire, Yorkshire and the Midlands.

A splendid stretch of golden sand extends for miles and this is a source of ecstasy for the little ones, and a haven of content, rest and enjoyment for their elders.

Popular as New Brighton has been for a considerable number of years past, it is as nothing compared with the extended popularity it has enjoyed since the construction of that great masterpiece, the New Brighton Tower, with its magnificent gardens covering an area of 35 acres.

Nowhere else in the Kingdom, or in fact the world, can be found so grand a sight, or a place so replete with amusements as the New Brighton Tower, for from the opening each day until the close, not a weary moment need be anticipated by intending visitors.

The means of access are now most convenient, frequent and direct boats from Liverpool Landing Stage during the season; a splendid service of electric cars via Seacombe, and at last but by no means least, the lately electrified system of the Mersey Railway Co., who run trains from Central Low Level or James Street Station (Liverpool), every few minutes.

The Grounds and Gardens, 35 acres in extent, present most beautiful natural features, and the designers must be complimented on the manner in which they performed their task. There is no appearance of artificiality; everything is true to nature, and herein lays the charm. Here will be found not merely the common attractions of so many holiday resorts, these gardens standing alone by the fact that within their boundaries every amusement that can be devised is provided for the entertainment of visitors.

With such advantages. natural and otherwise, it is only natural that the Tower should be visited by many hundreds of thousands every season.

On approaching the Tower Buildings, the main entrance will be seen leading to the Bazaar, Grand Tower Theatre, and the main staircase to the Ballroom, &c.

The Bazaar is occupied by numerous shops for the sale of fancy articles. Souvenirs & the entrances to the Theatre leading from either side of the Bazaar.

The Tower Theatre is one of the finest of its kind in the world. Seating accommodation is provided for 3,000 people, and the stage is one of the largest in England, having a proscenium opening of 45 feet, and a depth of 72 feet, and is so arranged that a full-sized circus can be placed upon it, which is often done during the season. At the back of the stage there is stabling for a large number of horses, also for wild animals, and all the arrangements, sanitary and otherwise, are on the latest improved plans.

The Season's Bookings for the Theatre include all the Drury Lane Dramatic Successes, Musical Comedies, and Grand Opera by the leading London Companies, and the variety programmes are rendered by the finest English, Continental, and American talent that can be procured, in addition to which a series of the latest Animated Pictures are depicted at every performance by the Tower scope. The curtain rises at 3 o'clock, and 7.45 pm daily, and on Bank Holidays at 2, 4.30 and 7.45 pm. There are no early door fees, but vast as the capacity of the Theatre is, there are times when the management cannot be accommodating all the patrons. Visitors may always rely on witnessing an entertainment that is clean, educational, elevating and amusing.

On ascending the main staircases, we find the Cloak Rooms, etc, and on the next floor to these is the magnificent Ballroom. This is one of the finest rooms in the Kingdom, and 1,000 couples can conveniently dance at one time on the beautiful parquet floor, which is supported by many thousands of springs, making dancing delightfully easy.

The artistic ornamentation of white and gold is most attractive, and attention should be given to the fine paintings in panels of the civic emblems of different Lancashire towns, which ornament the pillars. The renowned Tower Orchestra plays at frequent intervals, in fact dancing is continuous from 11 am to 10.15 pm daily. During the season this room is the scene of much gaiety, especially on the Scottish, Irish, Welsh and Territorial 'nights'. Dancing Competitions are held almost every week in addition to the Fancy Dress, summer, and Confetti Carnivals.

On the Ballroom Balcony there is seating accommodation for hundreds who may wish to watch the dancers.

Above the Ballroom is the Elevator Hall, surrounded by fancy shops, and fitted with numerous and highly amusing automatic machines. On entering the Hall, on one side is the shooting Jungle, and on the opposite side is the Aviary, comprising a large collection of beautiful birds, and the African Monkey House.

From the ground floor to the Elevator Hall auxiliary lifts are run all day free, and from the Elevator Hall the main lifts ascend to the

Top of the Tower; these lefts run every few minutes; a nominal charge is made for the ascent.

From the top of this magnificent structure, which stands 621 feet above the sea level, and is in fact the highest in the Kingdom, a view of landscape and seascape is to be obtained which lives long in the memory of those who witness it.

The noble river Mersey, with the fine line of Liverpool docks, stretches away north and south for miles, and from this great height the large ships look like toy vessels.

On the landward side is seen the Peninsula of Wirral, with the River Dee and the Welsh mountains in the distance. A more beautiful sea view is unobtainable in any part of the globe, nor can any spot be found where so many beautiful steamers may be watched for so many miles wending their way to or from distant countries; it is indeed a most imposing panorama and is appreciated to the fullest extent by all who see it.

Descending again to the gardens, the first thing that strikes the eye is the ornamental lake, and immediately opposite is the Japanese Cafe where refreshments of all kinds can be obtained at reasonable prices.

The old quarry (which is called the 'Happy Valley'), faces the Algerian Restaurant, with its large Rockeries planted with ferns and creepers, is another item of interest, and on a holiday it is a delightfully cool and pleasure resort; nestling in one corner is found the Parisian Tea Garden, where visitors map partake of light refreshments while listening to the Pierrots who perform at intervals during the day and evening. At the top of the Quarry will be seen amidst the trees Rock Point Castle, the first class restaurant.

Ascending the steps to the Old English Fair Grounds, we find first and foremost the ever-popular Electric Mountain Railway, the only one of its kind in the north, and which produces a most exhilarating effect on the passengers who travel round it; at the rear of this railway one may inspect the open-air Zoological Pens, whilst further on is the Shooting Gallery, and the Menagerie and Lion House. The Menagerie contains a most interesting and varied collection from all parts of the world, including the celebrated Lion 'Pasha', acknowledged to be one of the finest in captivity, and, in addition, the huge favourite elephant 'Punch'.

On the fair Grounds and throughout the amusement Park, in addition to those specially mentioned, will be found a numerous collection of side-shows, each one being a novelty and productive of much amusement.

Another great attraction is the Water Chute running from the level of the fairground into the ornamental lake below. It carries its passengers in specially built boats, which *cannot capsize,* down an incline some 130 feet long and launches them into the lake and then across to the landing place, causing a most exciting and thrilling sensation. The boats are then drawn back into position for another party, solely by electric power, in fact, the whole of the machinery connected with this wonderful establishment is electric, and all the electricity is generated on the premises, the plant being of more than 2,000 horse power.

At dusk each evening the whole gardens and buildings are transformed into a veritable fairyland by means of electric lights. Thousands of lamps are hung and festooned round the walks and trees, no fewer than 32,000 lamps being utilised for this purpose, while the inside of the buildings is one gorgeous blaze of light. The lamps are of different colours, and the beautiful effect is thus produced is extremely artistic.

The delight which is afforded by the excellent Tower Ground Orchestra, which gives a Promenade Concert each afternoon and evening, under such charming circumstances, is long remembered. We might write pages and pages in expatiating profusion of sights and novelties of the New Brighton Tower - its attractions are innumerable, its amusements limitless - and the surprised visitors finds it is impossible to see everything in one day.

Consequent upon the erection and popularity of this noble structure, New Brighton has itself reaped enormous benefits from the influx of visitors who pour in daily during the season, and from what was practically a small village has now sprung a town with fine residential property, as well as plenty of comfortable apartments at reasonable charges which compare favourably with similar seaside resorts, so that day or weekend visitors, or those desirous of staying longer, will find no difficulty in obtaining suitable accommodation.

This Guide would scarcely be complete unless mentions were made of the magnificent Sunday Evening Concerts which are given during the season. Nothing short of the best possible is the standard set up, and the arrangements for this year include the most famous available British and Foreign Military Bands, Orchestras, Choirs etc, while special engagements have been entered into vocal and instrumental artistes of world-wide repute. The Grand Tower Orchestra - forty in number - comprises the finest soloists of the Richter, Haile, Philharmonic, and other noted orchestras, and the concerts given weekly have earned the just reputation of being the finest in the provinces.

Shopping

Victoria Road

The Street with everything

Victoria Road became very popular due to its proximity to the Ferry Terminal and New Brighton Station which had opened in 1888. In Jonathan Bennison's 1835 map of the district the only building standing in Victoria Road was the New Brighton Hotel which looked out across sand-hills and scrub to the sea. The hotel-keeper in 1840 was a 63 year old widow named Isabella Graves who would later take up the tenancy of the Ferry Hotel at the bottom of Victoria Road a few years later. Isabella was landlady of the Ferry Hotel for a short period until she died in February, 1852, aged 75, and is laid to rest in St. Hilary's Churchyard. Thomas Longden would take up the tenancy of the New Brighton Hotel. Born in Bakewell, Derbyshire in 1802, he came to New Brighton from Liverpool in 1843. The hotel became prosperous in the mid 19th Century at a time when other buildings were emerging on Victoria Road. Langon remained proprietor until his death in

January, 1859, age 56. He was succeeded as proprietor by his widow, Mary. She successfully ran the hotel with her two daughters, Frances and Elizabeth, until their departure in the mid 1860's.

The hotel was once called *Lacey's* and today is known as *Peggy Gadfly's*, which is meant to refer to the original one-legged diver who used to draw the attention of passengers disembarking from New Brighton ferry-boats in the early part of the 20th Century by plunging into the river from the end of the Pier for the prospect of a few coppers. However, it would appear that Peggy's surname has been spelt incorrectly; his proper name being Peggy (or Pegleg) Gadsby.

The Ferry Hotel, at the base of Victoria Road, opened in c1850 and was in a favourable position to attract customers as it was the first building passengers would come across after alighting from their ferry-boat.

After Isabella Graves death her 26 year old great niece Ann Graves took over the tenancy of the Ferry Hotel. In 1857 the hotel was taken over by the notable architect Stephen Eyre who designed St. Albans Church with J.A Hanson in 1852-1853. Eyre remained at the hotel for 10 years and was succeeded by Miss Ann Tennant, a 30 year old, who changed the name of the hotel for a short period to 'Royal Hotel'. In 1869 Ann left to take up duties at the Magazine Hotel, Magazine Brow and was replaced by the onetime proprietor of the Queen's Hotel, Conway Street, Birkenhead, George Mason, who changed the title of the hotel to 'Royal Ferry Hotel'. George was a wealthy ship-owner and was elected a member of the Wallasey Local Board in 1870. After George retired in 1879 his son, Edward, became the proprietor until 1889 when he left to take up the tenancy of the Queen's Hotel in Conway Street and in 1892 was elected as a member of Birkenhead Borough Council, becoming Mayor of Birkenhead in 1897-1898. It is worth noting that Mason Street, off Victoria Road, and formally known as Black Diamond Street, takes its name from the family. Today the hotel is now residential flats but had recently been a nightclub called Chelsea Reach and Club Royale.

There were, of course, other hotels and public houses in Victoria Road such as the 'Commercial Hotel' (renamed the 'Ship Hotel' in the 1950's and latterly modified to the 'The Ship Inn'), the Lifeboat Hotel, the York Hotel and the Railway Hotel, which were initially private residences, shops and/or cafes that dated back to the 1840's and 1850's when the left hand side of the road, leading up from the Ferry, was first built up.

Prior to 1850 new buildings on the left hand side such as Fort Terrace, Rock View Terrace and St. George's Terrace were erected and were soon joined by Woodville Terrace and Crosby View during the 1850's. In 1860 the first building on the right hand side appeared and was erected on the corner of Waterloo Road and named Napoleon Buildings. It remained isolated for some time, being straddled upon both sides by sand hill and scrub, until the 1870's when Queen's Buildings and Imperial Buildings were built adjacent. During the 1860's Brighton Terrace and Seaforth View appeared on the left hand side, whilst Havelock and Richmond Buildings had joined Napoleon, Imperial and Queen's Buildings upon the opposite side by the late 1870's.

With the new buildings in place and cheap excursions made available for the working class, Victoria Road, in the 1870's, began to become quite popular with both visitors in the summer season and locals (there was an increase in both population of New Brighton and house building between 1850-1870). Wages were rising in real terms in this period and in 1871 saw the creation of the official Bank Holiday.

During the mid to late 19th Century a road that is a little more than a third of a mile in length had such a varied and well-balanced in commercial premises. There were:

Grocers and provision dealers, bakers, confectioners, wine and spirit merchants, fruiterers and greengrocers, fishmongers and poulterers, butchers, sweetshops and milk dealers;

Milliners, drapers, tailors, dressmakers and ladies' outfitters, hosier's and hatters, art and needlework dealers, dyers and cleaners, and boot and shoemakers;

Chemists, tobacconists, newsagents, stationers and booksellers, photographers and hairdressers;

Toys and fancy goods, china and glass dealers, ironmongers and chandlers, watchmakers and jewellers, cycle dealers, furniture dealers and antique dealers;

Two banks, a post office, printers, estate agents, dentists, chiropodists, circulating library and pawnbrokers;

Cafes, refreshment and tea-rooms, restaurants, pubs, hotels and boarding houses - as well as two private schools for boys and a billiard hall.

All of which were later joined by two cinemas in the first quarter of the 20th Century; namely the Court Picture House (or 'Picturedome' as it was originally called), which opened in 1912 and situated adjacent to Napoleon Building, between Windsor Street and Waterloo Road, and the Trocadero Picture House, opened in 1922 and located upon the right hand side of the road, near to its junction with Belmont Road.

Some of these businesses listed began a long tradition of trading in Victoria Road that dated back to the 1850's when the first shops appeared at the base of the road near to the Ferry Hotel. Gradually more shops extended up the road during the next two decades. By the last quarter of the 19th Century Victoria Road became a vibrant scene with shopkeepers who had traded in the resort for many years and were also the mainstay of the community.

Let's look at some of these traders in detail:-

Francis Storey was born in about 1845 in Ireland and opened his toy and fancy goods shop in New Brighton in the early 1870s. Later Francis would go on to represent the district in the Wallasey Urban Council, formed in 1894, which Francis was Chairman in 1903-1904, and on Wallasey Borough Council (founded in 1910). Between 1912-1913 Francis held the office of Mayor of Wallasey and in 1920 became the first Freeman of the Borough. Francis lived at 'Elmswood' in Atherton Street and even had a ferryboat named after him but sadly he passed away before the boat came into service. Meanwhile his second son John Gladstone Storey, born in New Brighton in 1882, would follow closely in his father's footsteps in the retailing business, as a fancy goods dealer in Victoria Road, and in politics as a local Liberal Councillor upon

235

Wallasey Council. John, too, being elected Mayor of Wallasey for the year 1929-1930.

Frank Fawcett Scott was born in Seacombe c1857 and opened his butchers at 38 Victoria Road (later renumbered as 83) in the late 1870s. Just like Francis Storey, Frank also served New Brighton on the Wallasey Urban Council and the Wallasey Borough Council. Frank also became Mayor of Wallasey between the years of 1917 to 1918.

In 1900, at number 90, we have Henry Spencer's drapers and small ware dealer. Henry was born in Liverpool in about 1828 and first opened his shop in Fort Terrace at the bottom end of Victoria Road in 1858, moving to newly built premises in Napoleon Buildings, on the corner of Waterloo Road. He then moved premises to the adjoining Queen's Buildings, when they were built in the 1870's, where the business remained until well into the 20th Century.

Mary Spicer ran a refreshment room at No. 3 Bickley Parade and is worth a mention due to the gruesome murder of her two sons by her partner Felix Spicer in May 1890. She was to leave New Brighton by the mid-1890s.

In 1865 is listed George Goodman, a Royal Navy pensioner, who was born in Saltash, Cornwall c1818. He arrived in New Brighton (via Brighton. Sussex) in about 1860 to take up duties as a coastguard. He soon abandoned this profession however in order to open a fishmonger and poulterers' shop. George was also to invest in other businesses in the resort such as becoming a proprietor of a temperance hotel and refreshment rooms in Victoria Road as well as operating a pleasure-boat service upon the river during the season. Also, George's wife, Mary Ann, who also was born in Saltash c1821, was similarly active in New Brighton's service industry at this time as a lodging house keeper, and she controlled a number of apartments in both Tollemache Street and Union Terrace during the 1870s and 1880s.

Also listed in 1865 is Whitham Bell's Grocers. Whitham was born in Colne, Lancashire c1829 and opened his shop in 1861. He soon incorporated the sale of wine, spirits, ales and porters. During the 1870s, Whitham's father, Thomas (born in Thornton, Yorkshire c1798) then took over the business with Whitham's younger brother, Lister (born in Addington, Yorkshire c1837). By the 1880s the shop was passed on to Lister's son, Lister M Bell, by which time Lister Snr was concentrating his attention on the alcohol section of the business. In the 1884 local trades' directory Lister Snr is listed as the proprietor of the Marine Hotel; a position he held until 1886 when the family appear to have left the resort. Their former premises on Victoria Road was later converted into the 'York Hotel', a popular hotelry which served customers until its closure in the mid 1960s.

Miss Alice Hind was born in Preston c1827 and was probably responsible for introducing the very first confectioners and refreshment rooms in Victoria Road in the early 1850s, and she ran this business successfully until 1871 when New Brighton born Henry A. Ducker (1851-1890) succeeded her. This business was later to become The Criterion Restaurant before operating as a public house in the mid 1950s. Alice continued to live at No.5 Victoria Road until 1904 when she moved to Tranmere. Henry's mother, Mary Ann Ducker (born Liverpool c1818) kept lodging houses and apartments in both Egerton Street and Tollemache Street during the 1850s, 60s and early 70s before branching out into retail trade with a toy dealers and fancy repository, in Rock View Terrace, Victoria Road in 1877. After ten years Mary turned her hand to the catering trade by opening two refreshment rooms in Victoria Road, which she continued to manage until 1898, the year of the last recorded reference to her in New Brighton.

In 1890, at No. 9, was the restaurant and dining rooms 'Whittaker', and was run by the founder's daughter. In 1859 Matilda Whittaker, born Northampton c1819, opened a 'tea, coffee and refreshment room' on Tea Pot Row with her husband Joseph (born Great Bolton c1809). In the early 1860s Joseph also set up a Photographic Room on the same premises. Sadly, Joseph died in 1865 but Matilda remained at Tea Pot Row, and, indeed, moved on to Woodville Terrace, Victoria Road in 1871 and opened a rather select restaurant and dining rooms which continued to operate most successfully until the early 20th Century. Her daughter Mrs Alice Hayes, born in Egremont c1846, took over the premises in 1885 but retained the "Whittaker" family name for business purpose.

Another established restaurant on Victoria Road in 1890 was Webster's at No. 6-7 (No. 13-15 when properties were later renumbered). Hannah Webster was born in Macclesfield, Cheshire c1817 and came to the resort in 1843 with her husband, Edward (born Yorkshire c1802). Hannah had six children who were all born in New Brighton. Hannah unfortunately became a widow in 1858 and at the same time was running a small refreshment room from their home at 'Blue Cottage', which stood detached and adjacent to Tea Pot Row near the shoreline. With children's age ranging from one to fourteen years old, Hannah managed to keep Blue Cottage going and even expanded the business in 1873 by opening a dining and refreshment room next door to Matilda's Whittaker's premises. Hence 'Webster's" soon became very popular eating place in the resort for visitors alike, and Hannah herself, by this time well into her eighties, was still at the helm at the turn of the 20th Century, after 40 years in the trade. Hannah's last reference in New Brighton was in 1900, but the new owners decided to keep the name of "Webster's" for another ten years due to the popularity of the restaurant.

Victoria Road in the 20th Century

Victoria Road

239

In the 1920's Victoria Road was quite a shopping area in itself, in addition to the the many restaurants and gift shops which catered for the visitors in the summer months.

The proprietor of the Royal Ferry Hotel in the 1920's was Charles Bagnall. A large round glass lantern hung over the main entrance. Not far away from there was, at one time, another public house called Mason's Ferry Hotel. Coming up Victoria Road was the confectioners owned by Mrs Alice Kingham which later became Fowden's Restaurant, and, next door, was Mrs Richard's who had a tobacconist shop. Four restaurants were next which caught the trade as the visitors came off the ferry boats. In later years we had Ducker's Criterion Cafe in this part of the road. Butler's was another popular cafe. Mrs. E. Horton opened a cafe at No. 11 which was continued on by William Horton, who opened other shops in the road in later years. There was three lots of people with the name of Humphreys in Victoria Road, the cafe (which later became Tom Peat's), the tobacconist and, next door, Henry Humphries Lifeboat Cafe. 'Madame Olga' set up a palmist and clairvoyant at No.16 in the 1930s.

The Commercial Hotel was next to 'Smith's Cafe', where Jack Kitchen was licensee and in later years the public house was renamed 'The Ship'. Peter Dudley's well-known restaurant was at No. 31. They were in business for many years and the business was carried on by Reg Duffey. The establishment was originally owned by Columbus De Giovannini, who then called it 'The Swiss Restaurant'. Mrs. Sarah Walker had the 'Liner Restaurant', later 'Evans Cafe'. 'Lawton's Cafe' opened later at No. 27. Mr. Moss had the jewellers and the Victoria Hall became the 'Empress Ballroom', under the care of Mr. Henry Kingham.

The amusement arcade on the ground floor came later. The 'Hamilton Cafe', which was run by the sisters Misses Lucy & Helen Heslim, was later taken over by Mr. Read. Miss Lee had the drapers shop with Lacey's bakery shop next door. Comberbach and Company were the wine and spirit merchants on the corner of Albert Street. Henry Smith was the ironmonger and George Bohm the German pork butcher. During the First World War the windows of George's shop was smashed and his sausages pulled all over the road. His son left school and on the first week at work fell off his cycle and fell under a bus and was killed.

Among the other shopkeepers on this side of the road was William Organ the tobacconists at No. 67 who were in business for many years and, next door, Mr. Mack who opened a shoe business in what was the old sweet shop. A Mr Harold Glue had the cafe where Woolworth's opened their store.

Mr Evans and his son had the drapers and next to the pork butchers run by Mr. Ellison was the York Hotel, where Bob Hodgson was landlord. On his death his wife, Wilheminia, took over the licensee and Noel Breeze became the popular landlord. Next door was Dewhurst the butchers, who later crossed the road to No. 84, taking over the premises of the British & Argentine Company. There were two fishmongers, Moloney and Gittins, which later became Sayers in one shop and the Maypole in the other. Samuel Henderson took over Arthur Latham's grocery business and proved to be one of the most popular grocers in Victoria Road. Leonard Harrison was another favourite grocer, he was at No. 115. Bert Taylor had the New Brighton Hotel for many years. The hotel was once owned by Leonard King and boasted two billiards tables. Huxley's had the hotel at one time, catering for private and commercial people, providing first class accommodation to motorists and cyclists. For 2s. 0d. they offered an excellent cuisine. Many years later, this large hotel was renamed the Neptune. Mr William Hardy had the jewellers higher up the road. He was a

243

member of the old Wallasey Council and served as Mayor of Wallasey between 1954-1955. He was in business for many years.

The Co-operative Society had their store and cafe at No. 103 and they later enlarged their premises by taking over other shops and carried out modernisation. Mr Payne from Wallasey Village was the manager. The premises became New Brighton's first large grocery store. The cafe was above and could seat one hundred and thirty people.

The Railway Hotel is on the corner of Grosvenor Road and was often referred to as 'Dunger's' because Tom Dunger was landlord. At the side of the building were steps leading down to a small bar with a long seat on the opposite side of the room. Among other shops were Edgar Hodgson the butcher, Knowles', Daveys and Chesters' the electrical and music shop who sold a wide selection of gramophone records. They also had a recording studio and Mr. Chesters played the electric organ at various functions.

Killitt's were the grocers on the corner of Rowson Street. A couple of other shops that were there in the 1950s were Mrs. Crosby's gift shop and Towneley Davies, the stationers.

On the right hand side of Victoria Road, starting at the bottom, was Storey's fancy goods shop on the corner which faced the drinking fountain by the ferry. On the site previously occupied the Bon Marche, this was a popular shop with the visitors because they could purchase a large variety of goods such as postcards, buckets and spades, celluloid's windmills, flags to put on top of sandcastle's, rock to take home and a host of 'present from New Brighton' gifts.

Above Storey's shop was the Avondale Cafe, which was owned by Mr. Rawlinson Peskett who also had the Douglas Cafe on the corner of Virginia Road, where the less well-off could take their own food, providing they bought a cup of tea.

There was the Waiting Room for the tramcars and the 'horse shoe' where the tramcars could turn around, and the track ran as far as the Tivoli Theatre.

Among the shops in this part of the road was Mr. William Brice the dairyman, George Parker's fish and chip shop, Edwin Wilson the outfitters and Joe Mumford the photographer who always had an interesting show of photographs in the window and Mr. Alfred Booth the chemist. The sweetshop at No.28, Eulah Ltd., always had a crowd outside as people watched in amazement as a machine with two arms stretched and folded soft toffee cream over and over again. Laid out in display in the window in front of the machine were all the little empty boxes which were used to put the creams in. At No. 34 was Arnold Chadwick's tobacconist who sold a good selection of pipes and leather goods and other gifts - he eventually moved across the road. His was the last shop in the road to sell goods with 'New Brighton' printed on.

George Stoneall the fisherman had his shop in the block for a long time and then there was Pegram's the grocers and Mr. Arthur Livesley was the dentist at No. 42 and No. 46 later became the 'The Sun Rise Cafe' after the Second World War. Triplett's the greengrocers was next to Barclay's Bank where Mr. J.L.W. Solley was the manager.

Though we are mainly dealing with shops in Victoria Road as well as looking at various hotels and public houses, it is, however, worth noting that next was the Trocadero picture house. It held nine hundred picture-goers and was opened by the Mayor of Wallasey, Alderman Augustine Quinn on 1st June, 1922 at 3.00 pm, and the first performance was presented that evening at 6.00 pm., the main feature being 'Perjury'. The cinema had a 'symphony orchestra', conducted by Mr. Besvoby. The cost of admission ranged from 6d. to 1s. 3d. The Gaumont British became owners in 1928 with Mr. Robin Jones as manager. Before it became a cinema it was the site of Albert Hall and a number of lock up garages. The first Baptist Pioneer Mission was started in these premises in 1890. The Albert Hall was also used as a billiards hall for a time before it was sold to the cinema company. The cinema closed down on 22nd September, 1956 and became a supermarket.

Mrs Sarah Higgerson had a cafe next to the picture house and on the corner of Belmont Road was the stationers and Avison's grocery at No. 68, then Emily Todd had the shop. Walter Buxton had the greengrocers and Mrs. Denham (milliner) and the chemist, Mr. John Crofts, was on the corner of Richmond Street. The opposite corner was where the Davies Brothers, who were ironmongers, had their shop. This shop became T. Gribbon's, the popular greengrocer. Mr. Charles Fry had a branch of his pawnbrokers business by the British and Argentine Meat Company, with Mr. Douglas Murdoch as manager. Mr. Brown was the greengrocer and S. Panter Brick was the draper next to the tobacconist. Lunt's the bakers were next to the Court Picture House, which was run by the Mersey Halls Limited. It had opened on 16th December, 1912 and was one of the smallest cinemas in Wallasey; Mr. C. G. Scarborough was the manager in the 1930s. It was not a very popular picture house as regards as attracting people from other parts of the town but it came into its own when Mr. Whilma Wilkie of the New Brighton Palace bought it and completely modernised the cinema, putting in the very latest equipment but after a long period of success, like other cinemas, it was forced to close on 22nd March, 1969.

Mrs. Martha Fitzgerald was the postmistress at the New Brighton Post Office. This post office used to open on Sundays between 8.30 am to 10 am. Mr. James Theckston ran the chemist shop next door and during the First World War he was the postmaster at the Post Office. Mr. Wilberforce was a chemist on the other side of the road at one time and he crossed the road and opened a business on this side.

Higher up were other shops, including Worthington's the tobacconists, with a hairdressers behind. Mrs. Dickson, the ladies outfitters, Bill Borland (boot maker), Borland's fruit shop and Mrs, Hess (millinery). Perhaps this part of the road should have had the name of Bank Corner as there were three banks at one time. On the corner was the red brick built 'City and Midland Bank' and the 'Liverpool Bank and 'Martins Bank' on the other (now the *Tallulah's* bar). On the opposite side of the road as one went up the hill was the Manchester and Liverpool District Banking House.

The 1970s would start to see the decline in Victoria Road as far as being highly commercial with the fall in both local and tourism trade. Most people either wanting to travel to town centres for shopping or, during the summer months, go on holiday abroad where the weather was more reliable. Many of the household names that generations had grown up with started to see these long established shops close.

The Royal Ferry Hotel would soon be transformed into a night club but during this time Leonard Patten was the licensee. Eric Rowlands was the manager of the Criterion, replacing Mr. G. Wilson, and Bob Collins Cafe was at No. 11. Sheffield Restaurant was at No. 17 with Mr. J. Jou the proprietor and sisters Christina and Jean Randles were licensee of the Ship Hotel until 1976 when Alan Smith then became the landlord. Continuing along we had Lawton Confectioners, Mrs Taylors Toy Shop and the long established Duffey Restaurant, owned by Reginald and Amelia Duffey who had been at No. 31 Victoria Road since the early 1920s when first opened by Mrs. Mary Duffey. Next door was Paddy's Cafe, then Europa Cafe under the management of Mr. Lee White. The Empress Snack Bar & Restaurant was once at No. 37

but by 1972 had become the Golden Sovereign which advertised the latest fruit machines, pin tables and children's rides. During the summer season the Golden Sovereign opened every day from 9am but in the winter only opened at the weekend. By the early 1970s Arnold Chadwick's Tobacconists had closed after more than 30 years of trading and the shop was replaced with Colley's Gift Shop. Next door was Edith Morris Drapers, then the New Delhi Restaurant with Tracadero Snack Bar on the corner of Albert Street with Edward Clark as the manager.

Woods Grocers once stood on the opposite corner of Albert Street in the late 1960s. Bohm Pork Butchers continued trading into the 1970s as well as Organ's Newsagents. Mack's Shoe Repairer was next door, then Woolworths at No. 71-73, which had opened a store in Victoria Road in the early 1950s. The grocers Four Seasons was at No. 77 and Hammer's Amusements was at No. 83. Sayers had a shop at No. 85, the Wine & Spirits Co-Op was at No.89 and on the corner of Mason Street was Barclays Bank. All

250

these buildings between Albert Street and Mason Street have since been demolished and new housing now occupies the site.

The Neptune Hotel stood on the opposite corner of Mason Street and John Holland was the landlord in the 1970s. The Neptune would later change its name to Lacey's and then Peggy Gadfly's

As we move along up Victoria Road we had Henry Jones Bookmakers, Hardy's Jewellers, Grocery Co-Op and Silver Slipper Restaurant was at No. 111. E.Price Butchers was at No. 115 and Gribbon'a Fruiterers & Greengrocers was on the corner of Grosvenor Road.

Landlord of the Railway Hotel in the early 1970s was Thomas McCabe who left in 1980 and Ken Pickett became the new proprietor. Other shops included Guest the Butchers, Lillibet Children's Wear who were No. 125 and Cosmo Cafe was next door. Hutton had the newsagents and then there was Lune Cleaners. Further along was Chesters the electrical engineers. In the late 1960s Mr. Ashman was a Turf Commission Agent on the

251

corner with Rowson Street. A Turf Commission Agent was someone who placed bets on behalf of owners or trainers with bookmakers.

Starting from the bottom end of Victoria Road, on the left hand side, was Wallasey Power Boat & Ski Club which had been Horton's Corner Shop. Brice the Caterers was at No.6 and next door was Samuel Worthington's Fancy Goods. At No. 10 was Maxim's Restaurant and further up the road was Gregon's Chemist. In the 1960's Kowloon Restaurant had been at No. 65 but in the early 1970s had moved to No. 28. It's neighbour was the long established Midland Cafe run by the Creedon family who had been trading in the resort since the 1930s. No. 38 was Albert Cox and his Fancy Goods shop and at No. 40 was George Stoneall Fishmongers who had been trading on Victoria Road for fifty years.

In 1966 Jardines Confectioners use to be on the corner of Belmont Road at No. 64 but moved by the 1970s to No. 70. Costigans were at No. 68. Cooke Chemist was on the corner of Richmond Street and Stubb's Hardware, who sold garden equipment, stood at No. 78 on the opposite corner. The confectioners Golden Tea Pot was next door. No. 84 was Dewhurst the butchers. Further along, after Windsor Street, was Kendall's newsagent then Peter Antoni's Hairdressers who also had an establishment in Seaview Road. Mr R. Wilberforce had the chemist and on the corner of Waterloo Road was New Brighton Taxi's.

The other side of Waterloo Road is the Post Office and next door was Band's Fruiterers and Greengrocers. Further along was another Fruiterers & Greengrocers - J.W Moss. The self service launderette, Benedix, was at No. 118 and on the corner of Rowson Street was the Midland Bank.

Public Houses

The Magazines Pub

'The Magazine Hotel' was built in 1759, but over the years several alterations have been carried out. The pub was originally called 'The Black Horse' and the old house plate had the initials of R.T and the date. The hotel has a concealed cellar which was used by the old Press Gang. There was once a cock-fighting pit behind the hotel which had circular wooden seating for sailors and locals who would arrange and bet on bird fights. The Mags was often frequented by top-hatted gentlemen, city clerks and shipping people, many of whom arrived in horse-drawn cabs and were known as 'bay window customers'.

Various landlords included Charles Lear in 1861, Ann Tennant, 1872, Jim Lawson, 1884, Joseph Minsell, 1890, Catherine Ellen Hillier, 1911 and Percy Hall in 1938.

The Pub had to have an urgent refurbishment in 2010 following an electrical fire. Fortunately, very little History was lost to the flames. Two witch's broomsticks used to hang from the ceiling near the main fireplace. According to local legend, if something were to happen to either of them, something bad would happen to the Pub. One of the broomsticks was stolen just before the fire. The remaining one is now re-instated, further out of reach, and has a toy witch perched on it. Here is the full story regarding the fire.

The landlords of a Merseyside Pub which was almost destroyed by a fire believe a mysterious curse is to blame. The blaze at the 250-year-old Magazine Hotel in Wallasey caused £200,000 worth of damage and left managers Linda and Les Baxendale living in a caravan for three months. A small fabric witch figure which hung from the ceiling of the main bar was stolen two nights before the fire. And with a History of accidents befalling those who dared to touch it, the couple are convinced the two are connected.

The official cause was a power surge which blew up the Pub's fuse box, starting a fire. Linda, 59, said: "Part of the History of the Pub is the two witches and a little devil, all made from brown felt, which were hanging by the bar. "No-one knows exactly how long they were there and we don't know who gave them to the Pub but we think they were there for at least 100 years." They were covered in cobwebs and dust because we were told that if anyone touched those bad things would happen to them." The Baxendales have managed the Magazine Hotel, known locally as the Mags, since 2000 and Linda also ran the Pub between 1980 and 1993 with late partner Phil. When they first moved in they received an anonymous phone call warning them not to touch the witches. She said: "We found out that a decorator took them down while he was working here in the 1970s and then was involved in a serious car accident at the top of the road. "Phil once happened to touch the witch by accident and the following day he fell through a trapdoor leading to the cellar and broke his collarbone.

"Someone else fell over the following week and broke both his knees. It's spooky."Linda says she was convinced something terrible would happen after she learned about the theft. She said: "One of my bar staff, Charlie, saw a man take the witch from the ceiling on the Friday night and run out. He wasn't a regular because they all know the story.

"I suppose I am superstitious because I used to say to the witches 'I tell people not to touch you so look after me' but when I found out one had gone I said 'oh God something bad's going to happen now. "We live above the Pub and on Sunday we woke up about 7.45am to the sound of smashing downstairs. "I thought someone had broken in and was using a baseball bat until Les went downstairs and found it was a fire. "It was terrifying. If it wasn't for the prompt response of the fire service the Mags might have burned to the ground."

The remaining witch and devil were found in the scorched remains of the bar after the fire on April 18 but Linda says they have since vanished. A friend bought the couple a replacement witch from Pendle which now hangs in their place. They are celebrating the Pub's re-opening with a beer and cider festival next week which will include a special brew, Witches Revenge. Linda said: "What happened was so strange that I thought I'd better put the new witch up – just in case."

The Telegraph Inn

'The Telegraph Inn', which dates back to 1841. 'The Telegraph' is said to have functioned as a kind of ship's chandlery or store initially, and the name of the pub is probably derived from its operations in the early days. With its natural elevated position the premises were used to send telegraph messages by means of flags to ships upon the river and in Liverpool Bay. Old maps and local directories clearly show that the building was trading as a beer house in the 1850's and by the 1870's 'The Telegraph' was operating as a kind of grocer's store with the added facility to sell beer. The owner at this time was James Milnes who passed away in 1880 leaving his widow, Caroline, 51, to retain the business. During the 1890's Caroline employed her son, James, and his wife Elizabeth, as 'grocers assistants' which gave them good experience because by 1900 Elizabeth was listed as the owner. Remarkably, it is not until 1904 that 'The Telegraph' is granted as licensed premises. By the outbreak of World War One the premises was under the management of Mr. James Todd and for more than forty-years was to remain in the Todd family, ending with Mrs. Annie Todd in the 1950's.

The Boat House Hotel

'The Pilot Boat-house', usually known as 'Boat-house', was originally built in 1747. It was called the "Pilot Boat House" because a small boat belonging to the Pilotage was kept at the back of the inn. Post Mortem's of those who were found drowned in the river were held in the public house. The Pilot Boathouse mainly catered for the less-to-do artillery men from the Battery and workmen who were engaged in promenade building. It is said that the Pilot Boat's saloon reeked of thick-twist tobacco, that the floor was covered in sawdust and that the numerous and commodious spittoons were well blessed.

The old date plate had the initials of 'B' (surname) and G.M (Christian names) and the date of 1747, under which was another date of 1876 and L.R, and at the bottom was APL. It suggests that rebuilding took place in April 1876. The building was enlarged with the entrance on the corner. The older building was left and was quite quaint in its way. Richard Dean was a long time serving landlord who was noted in 1812 and again in 1861. In 1900 John Turner was the landlord, followed by John Miles Jones at the time of the First World War. By 1938 Charles Frederick Portlock was the licensee.

New Brighton Hotel

A grander affair then the Boathouse stood at the bottom of Magazine Lane near the shore. Variously known as the Liscard Hotel (Tithe Map, 1841), the New Brighton Hotel and the Stanley Arms, it enjoyed a rather chequered history. In late 1853 Dr. Poggi opened it as New Brighton College and it flourished until October 1862 when a great fire destroyed part of the building (some 'history' books note the date incorrectly of 1864). Dr Poggi was also a fellow countryman and friend of the Italian general and politician, Giuseppe Garibaldi, whose two sons Menotti and and Ricciotti were among Dr. Poggi's first pupils at New Brighton College. After the fire the building was used as a Bakers before being demolished in 1899. The site today is Magazine Promenade though there is a Victorian/Edwardian cast-iron columned shelter where Vale Drive meets Magazine Promenade called Dr. Poggi's Shelter.

New Brighton College

Liverpool Mercury, Wednesday 29th October, 1862

We are now enabled to lay before our readers full particulars of the disastrous fire at New Brighton College on Monday night, the announcement of which appeared in yesterday's Mercury. *The*

*premises, consisting of a capaolous house, with stabling, and the
necessary out-buildings, were situated midway between Egremont
Ferry and New Brighton, and were well known to all frequenters pf
the Cheshire shore. At the time of the outbreak of the fire there
were in the house besides the family of Dr. Poggi, the principal,
Miss Jones, the family governess; Messrs. Cooper and Pawson, the
resident masters, Mr. Pollesfen. a gentleman commercially
connected with Liverpool, but residing with Dr. Poggi; 24 resident
pupils, and several servants. About seven o'clock the attention of
one of the female domesties was attracted to the upper part of the
building by a strong smell as of fire, and on proceeding to the
corridor leading to the attics and to one or two lumber rooms she
found it densely filled with smoke which strengthened her
suspicion that something was wrong. She instantly informed one of
the pupils, and they were proceeding in company to alarm Dr.
Poggi, when on the stairs they met Miss Jones, the governess, with
one of the younger members of the family, whom she was escorting
to bed, and informed her of what they had seen. With great
prudence they sent for the doctor, who was seated with Mrs. Poggi
in the sitting room (that lady only being confined only a fortnight)
and stated that he was wanted; immediately he was acquainted
with the facts he rushed upstairs and found the flames pouring
from one of the attics and a lumber room opposite, so completely
severing all communication with the other rooms on the corridor
that any attempt to recover the property which they contained
would have been alike futile and dangerous. On the stairs Dr.
Poggi met five working men whose attention on the outside had
been arrested by the bright light in the upper stories of the house,
and by the volumes of smoke which poured from the windows, and
who had rushed in to render what assistance they could.*44

---

44 Liverpool Mercury, Wednesday 29th October, 1862

It was, however, quickly discovered that the fire had obtained too strong of the promises to be easily reduced, and attention was consequently turned first to safety of the inmates and then to the recovery of such property as was within reach. The doctor conveyed the news to the inmates, and speedily every member of the family, including Mrs. Poggi and her infant, was placed beyond the reach of harm, and the pupils were scattered. The painful position in which Mrs. Poggi was placed might under such circumstances have occasioned the most serious consequence, but Charles Holland, Esq., a magistrate and a near neighbour, with a sympathy which reflects upon him the highest credit, took Mrs. Poggi and her eight children, with the governess and nurse, to his residence, which they still make their home. Long before this time, crowds of persons, attracted by the flames, had assembled on the spot, and there, arranged and superintended by Mr. Holland, proceeded to remove from the lower part of the premises all the furniture contained in the morning rooms, nursery, library, and dining room. Of course in the excitement and the haste much of the valuable property was damaged and rendered comparatively worthless. The rooms mentioned were, however, cleared, and amongst the property saved is the valuable library of books. This done, an effort was made to save the property from the next floor, but with the exceptions of a few articles from the bedrooms it was found impossible to rescue any of the valuable property on that floor. The flames had previously burst through the roof, and the weight of the burning joists and timbers falling above the heads of the men engaged on the second floor rendered further efforts extremely dangerous, and they were therefore most reluctantly compelled to abandon the task. The property rescued from the burring pile was removed to the Fort, where it was left in safe custody, but it formed an insignificant portion of the furniture of so large a house, and will be of little value.

At an early period an engine from Birkenhead arrived on the spot, and began to throw a limited quantity of water on the fire, the supply being exceedingly short; but from the first it was felt that all hope beyond that of saving the mere walls was visionary and groundless. It continued, however, to play until three o'clock yesterday morning, when the fire was sufficiently subdued to enable the firemen to return to their homes. The fire burnt with great fury during the early part of the evening, the flames being distinctively visible from the landing stages; indeed, it was at first thought that some vessel lying in the river had ignited, and one of the steam tugs put off to render assistance. but came back when the nature of the conflagration was ascertained. The fire continued to burn throughout the night, and was raging in the cellars even yesterday afternoon, but no further damage was apprehended. Nothing remains but the bare walls of the building, which are in a very dangerous state, if we except the back kitchen and stable, which was preserved from destruction by the efforts of the firemen, who obtained a supply of water from the premises of Mr. J.B. Hughes, a short distance from the spot.

The house, which belongs to a Mr. Kenyon, living near Warrington, is insured, and Dr. Poggi's lost is fully covered by insurance in the Royal Office. The furniture of all the bedrooms, the linen, the wearing apparel of Dr. Poggi and all his family, together with every article which the maters. governess, and 24 pupils possessed, have been destroyed, not one of them having saved even a change of clothing. In addition to this loss, Dr. Poggi only two months since expended £75 in painting and repairing the house so as to render it a more comfortable home for the gentlemen committed to his case. A body of the Cheshire county police from Wallasey, under the charge of Inspector Rowbottom and Sergeant Hindley, were present, and rendered valuable and efficient service, and the greatest praise also is due to the labouring men and sailors, who vied with each other in striving to save from the devouring element as much as possible of the valuable property. To Mr. Holland the reverend gentleman feels laid under great obligation, for the prompt and gentle-manly offer of his residence as a home for himself and family; nor are his friends less cheerfully accorded to Mrs. Murdock, of Manor House, and to J.B. Hughes. Esq., who jointly undertook the charge of the pupils.

The origin of the fire has not been positively ascertained, but there is every reason to think it was occasioned by an explosion of gas in one of the upper rooms. Dr. Poggi having only a few moments before the alarm was given been somewhat startled by the diminution of light in the sitting room; that supposition is also strengthened by the strong smell of gas which pervaded the house when Dr. Poggi first ascended the stairs; but how it became ignited will probably ever remain a mystery. The fire was still smouldering in the cellars of the house yesterday afternoon, but no further mischief was apprehended.

Sport & Leisure

New Brighton Vale Park

In 1830 the area of land now occupied by Vale Park was formerly an estate called Liscard Vale, this being the origin of the park's name. The estate was later divided, with the second estate being named The Woodlands, now recalled by Woodland Drive, the Road situated at the park's Western boundary. In 1898, at a cost of £7,750, both estates were purchased by Wallasey Urban District Council, with the intention of providing a 'lung' or breathing space for an increasing population. The combined grounds opened as Vale Park on 20th May 1899.

Vale House built c1830 was originally a family home possibly belonging to a Cotton broker and was later extended. The family of Charles Holland, a Liverpool businessman and Wirral JP, lived here for over 50 years. Charles Holland travelled widely, returning with Botanical specimens and many of the trees now gracing the park were planted by his gardeners. For much of the 20th century Vale House accommodated the park staff, though it lay disused for some years the Friends of Vale Park encouraged the council to restore it. It opened as a community centre in 1993.

William Grinsell Burston was the first Head Gardener of Vale Park, though his title was Curator, perhaps reflecting the knowledge and expertise of someone in this position at the end of 19th century. He came to Liscard Vale as Head Gardener in 1890. When the estate was taken over by the council; 'W.G' (as he was always known) stayed on and became Curator to the new Vale Park. Most of the laying out of the park, arranging the flower beds and paths, etc was undertaken by him. He was considered to be an expert Botanist, and spent many hours sorting seeds and discussing rare plants with specialists from Liverpool museum. W.G. died at Vale Park House in 1918.

Ernest Burston, W.G's youngest son worked as a Vale Park gardener between 1918 and 1946 living with his wife in Vale House which had been converted into two flats following his father's death. In 1926 a Doric-columned bandstand was constructed and played host to brass band concerts as it continues to do so to this day.

Vale Park, showing New Band Stand, New Brighton

The park eventually passed into the hands of Wirral Borough Council and has seen some restoration over the years, mainly due to the efforts of The Friends of Vale Park. A successful application for funding in 1999 enabled restorative work to the Bandstand to be undertaken. Works included; waterproof treatment to the dome roof and rainwater channels, refurbishment of performers changing facility, re-laying of staging, exterior painting and re-cladding to the rear elevation to improve security of the structure.

During 1999 funding was also sought to replace the entire perimeter fencing of the bandstand site to both better secure and define the space as a performance/events area. This work coincided with the parks centenary celebrations, the date of which is commemorated in steelwork topping the gate entrance into the area.

The park is still open to visitors and Vale House now sports a tea room which offers a relaxing view across the flower gardens which each year are beautifully presented.

Lantern Parade New Brighton

Liverpool Mercury Tuesday, 1st September, 1896

The spirit of carnival has developed in this district to a large extent during the past few years, and the latest example, a lantern parade and fancy dress festival at New Brighton, Egremont, and Seacombe last evening, proved one of the prettiest gatherings of the kind which has been held. Fortunately for the success of the festival, the weather, which is, perhaps the chief factor to success in outdoor affairs of this nature, was favourable until the proceedings were well over, and the ladies and gentlemen in fancy dress who formed the procession, and the thousands of spectators who thronged the line of route, were enabled to enjoy the proceedings in comparative comfort. The object of the carnival was to help the funds of the Liverpool and New Brighton Lifeboat Institute, and numerous willing volunteers gave aid in various ways to make the festival a success. The start was made at dusk from the Horse Shoe at New Brighton Pier, and the procession was divided into sections, each of which was headed by a band. Among the several hundred cyclists who formed part of the procession, some exceedingly pretty, striking, and grotesque characters were to be noticed, while the members of the various harrier, athletic, and swimming clubs and minstrel troupes, who were indefatigable with their collecting boxes, were attired in every variety of fanciful and humorous costume. The hundreds of coloured lanterns and lights, with which the vehicles and cycles were adorned, gave a lively and picturesque appearance to the scene as the procession slowly made its way along the appointed route. The first section was led by Chief Superintendent Hindley, on horseback, a number of outriders, the local fire brigade, the 1st Cheshire and Caernarvonshire A.V Band, the New Brighton lifeboat and crew, drawn by five horses, on a lorry; the 1st Cheshire Bugle Band, and the chairman's, secretaries', and treasurer's carriage. The second

272

section was headed by the Gleam of Sunshine Band and the ladies' committee carriage, the third by the Workshops for the Blind Band, and the fourth by the Moreton Brass Band. The route taken was along Victoria Road, Rowson Street, Seabank Road, Ling Street (Egremont), Brighton Street, Seacombe Ferry, St. Paul's Road, Church Road, Victoria Road (Seacombe), Liscard Road, Liscard Village, Rake Lane and Upper Brighton, back to the starting point. A feature of the procession, which showed good organisation, was the prompt start at the advertised time, and the avoidance of delays and stoppages which, as a rule, characterise undertakings of this kind. The tradesmen of New Brighton and Seacombe materially helped the success of the spectacle by a liberal display of bunting and coloured lanterns, and the discharge of fireworks. Prizes were awarded for the best turnouts, both harriers and cyclists, as well as for the best collectors. These were as follows:-

Cyclists45 – Best Illuminated Machine: 1. W. Ridley (West Kirby), "Sultan"; 2. F. Gell (Liscard), "Eastern Prince." Neatest Costume: 1. B.Hands (New Brighton), "Japanese." Most Comic: 1. T.Smith (New Brighton), "Old Lady", 2. A.Medalf, "Irish Sailor." Most Original: 1. H.Silcock (West Kirby), "Neptune up to date." Neatest Character Dress (lady): 1. Miss Alice Crouch, "Italian Flower Girl." 2. Miss. Carson, "Little Red Riding Hood." Best Tableaux: 1. R.Jenkins, "Winter," 2. T.Bell and E.Howard as "Weary Willie and his Wife on the Road." Best Illuminated Tandem: 1 W. And A.Crouch, "Duke's Cameo"; 2. Brothers Soloman, "Darkies." A special prize was accorded to Mr. W.R. Richards for his representation of the famous Sussex cricketer, Prince Ranjitsinhji. The judges of the above events were Messrs. F.T Parry, R.R Ellis, J.Greetham, J.F Hughes, and F.H Smith. The harriers' turnout was none the less attractive, and competition in

---

45 Liverpool Mercury Tuesday, 1st September, 1896

273

this respect was exceptionally keen. The following were the wards in regard to this particular section :-

Most Comic Harrier: H. Walker (Xaverian Darkies), "Negro Lady." Neatest Costume: J.P Breckenridge, "Louis XVI." Most Original Costume: 1. J.F Walker, "Light Railways"; 2. E.N.T Mitchell, "King Winter"; 3. H.Knight, "Tiny." Neatest Dressed Boy Under 14: J.A Salisbury, "Black and White." Neatest Dressed Girl Under 14: Francis Drew. "Gipsy." Neatest Dressed on Horseback: I.S.P Chambers, "Indian"; 2. J.H Scott, "Jockey." Neatest Dressed Marshall on Horseback: S. Lowe, "Hussar." Most Comical Dressed Marshall on Horseback: "Clown", F. Gibson. Special Prizes: Miss Phillipps, "Harvest"; Master A.E Walker, "Mornington Cannon"; J. Bushell, "Dick Turpin"; "Neopolitan." Miss Agnes Benson: "Negro Clown," M.M Robertson"; "Red Indian," A. Hulme; "Charley's Aunt," H. Hooton; "Acrobat," E. Battersby; "Dashing Cavalier," --- Colley; "Upside Down," E. Bagot, "Illuminated Premises" (extra prize), Mrs. Tate, 51 Brighton Street, Seacombe. Prizes were given to shopkeepers for special displays, and these were accorded to – 1. Mrs. Outram, Victoria Road, New Brighton; 2 Mrs. Dale, Brighton Street, Seacombe; 3. Mrs. Huxley, New Brighton Hotel. In connection with the affair, Old English Sports were held on the shore at New Brighton in the afternoon. The following were the results:-- Boy's race: 1. Claude Tregenze; 2. J. Leach; 3. J. Thornton. Girls Race: 1. Maud Jones; 2. Florrie Jones; 3. Alberta Clegg. Egg-and-Spoon Race: Margaret Harrison. Sack Race: 1 J. Daniels; 2. J. Leach. Donkey Race: Mrs Stephenson. Climbing the Greasy Pole: Thomas Hayes. The following were the chief officials of the parade :-- President, Mr. Charles Birchall; chairman, Mr. J.W Brien; vice-chairman, Messrs F.H Smith, R.B. Robertson, J. Greetham, J. Bennett, J. Ward Dale and R.R Ellis; honorary treasurer Mr. C. Huxley; and general honorary secretary, Mr. John F. Walker.

The New Brighton Tower & Fairground

Back before I was born New Brighton was a "Great" British Seaside Resort. It was more popular than Blackpool, offered many things to enjoy, and at one point in time had the highest tower in Britain. By the time I was born in 1981 it was all gone and as if it never existed. How did a booming leisure resort disappear virtually overnight?

First of all we must mention the Tower, which really was a truly remarkable landmark that featured on the New Brighton waterfront at the end of the 19th century, which expressed the rise of the small seaside town in to a busy recreational resort.

Liverpool Mercury, Monday 10th February, 1896

There can be no doubt that the efforts being put forward by public bodies and private individuals to make New Brighton one of the most attractive seaside resorts in the north will meet with the approval, not only for visitors, but of the majority residents in the district. We announced in our columns a few weeks ago that a scheme had been decided upon for the establishment of a pleasure resort in New Brighton on lines somewhat similar to those at Olympia in London. That project has now assumed definite shape, and the site - the estate of the late Captain Molyneux on Rock Point - has been secured by a company (at the head of which is Mr. R.P. Houston, M.P.), who have paid a deposit of over £2000 to the trustees of the property46. The grounds, as already indicated, are about 500 yards to the south of the pier, and are bounded on the est. side by the river. The promenade, which is to be extended from the Magazines, Egremont, to New Brighton, will give convenient access to the grounds, whilst an upper entrance will be provided in Rowson Street. One of the principal features of the scheme will be the Eiffel Tower, such as was erected in Blackpool, and it will be interesting to the public to know that at the present times excavating operations are in progress in order to prepare the foundations of the tower. That the scheme is one of immense proportions will be readily realised when it is stated that it is the intention of the company to spend something like a quarter of a million of money in providing grounds, in which will be found attractions of every conceivable character. We understand that the company have also acquired the lease and interest of the Royal Ferry Hotel, close by the pier, with which establishment, we believe, Captain Walters has for some been connected. With a gentleman of enterprise like Mr. Houston at the head of affairs, it is expected that the scheme will be a great a success. There seems to be no reason to fear that the pleasure grounds will injure the Palace, for there will doubtless be generous support given to both places by the increased number of visitors who are sure to find

---

46 Liverpool Mercury, Monday 10th February, 1896

their way to New Brighton. It should be added that the new company have spared no pains to secure every possible advantage in order to make the scheme as popular as possible. Indeed, it is stated that they recently approached the Wallasey District Council with a request that the present landing pier might be removed to a position directly opposite the grounds. This request they backed up with an offer to build the new pier if the council approved of the idea. That matter, however, we find, fall through, as the council could not see their way to interfere with the present position of the landing pier, which they pointed out was directly in a line with Victoria Road, the principal thoroughfare of the district.

The statistics of the Tower when it was complete

- *Start Date: 22nd June 1896*
- *Completion Date: 1900 (exact date unknown)*
- *Cost: £120,000*
- *Materials: over 1,000 tons of steel*
- *Height: 567 feet 6 inches to the top of the flagstaff*
- *Height above sea level: 621 feet.*
- *Architects: Maxwell and Turk of Manchester*

- *Builders: Handy sides and Company of Derby*

The New Brighton Tower was patterned on the world-famous Eiffel Tower in Paris. It all started when a newly formed company called The New Brighton Tower and Recreation Company Limited, with a share capital of £300,000 decided to purchase the Rock Point Estate of over 20 acres. The Tower was to be 544 feet high, with Assembly Hall, Winter Gardens, Refreshment Rooms and layout with a cycle track. The Tower was to be more elegant than Blackpool's. Shares were £1 each and the Tower would be made of mild steel.

During the construction of the Tower six workmen were killed and another seriously injured either though falls or accidents. On completion the Tower was the highest building in the country. Soon after the Tower was opened a young man threw himself off the balcony to be the first suicide from the building. Four lifts took the sightseers to the top of the structure at a cost of 6d. From there you could see for miles around including the Isle of Man, Great Orme's Head, part of the Lake District and the Welsh Mountains.

279

The Tower is said to have attracted around half a million people in the year.

Along with the Tower, a ballroom was built and was one of the largest in the world, with a sprung floor and dance band stage. The orchestra had as many as 60 players and well over 1,000 couples could dance without overcrowding, it was decorated in white and gold, with emblems of various Lancashire towns. There was a balcony; with seats to watch the dancers below and behind this was an open space where couples could learn to dance. There was also a fine Billiard Saloon with 5 billiard tables and above the Ballroom was a Monkey House and Aviary in the Elevator Hall, there was even a Shooting Gallery!

Mayor's Ball at the New Brighton Tower

As well as the Tower and ballroom the area was surrounded by a Tower Gardens complex. The Tower Gardens covered something like 35 acres in all, with a large Japanese Cafe at the lakeside, where real Gondoliers had Venetian Gondolas. There was also a fountain and seal pond in the old quarry, with its rockery. Then there was a Parisian Tea Garden where one could have a cup of tea

281

while watching the Pierrots. Towards the river end, there was an outdoor dancing platform which held a thousand dancers, where the Military Band played, stating at 9 o'clock in the morning in the height of the season. Above the dance floor was a high wire for tightrope walking, without any safety net. The tightrope walker was a man by the name of James Hardy, who had a bet with another man that he could walk across the rope with a girl on his shoulders. He won his bet when he carried the barmaid from the Ferry Hotel across his back which was quite an interesting tale to have been told.

There were also other light orchestras which played here and at variety performances in the theatre in the afternoon. A good restaurant called "The Rock Point Castle" was situated amongst the trees, with lovely pathways to wander around. The Tower grounds had their own private Police force of up to 15 men would parade around and keep order.

However the tower did not last for long, after the outbreak of the First World War, the public were no longer allowed to venture up to the top of the Tower for military reasons. In the war years the steel structure was neglected and became rusty through lack of maintenance and the cost of renovating was more than the owner could afford so sadly this became the beginning of the end of the

283

tower. The top portion of the structure commenced to be dismantled on 7th May 1919 and was completed in June 1921. The brick portion comprising of the Ballroom and Theatre remained, together with the turrets. During the Second World War the basement was used as a communal air-raid shelter.

The Fairground remained with the Ballroom and other surrounding features until its final fate during the fire of 1969. The Old English Fairground was on a higher level which, in later years, became the motor coach park. The Himalayan Switchback Railway was a great favourite, as was the water chute, with the boats travelling down at speed into the lake. The Railway had previously been at the Brussels Exhibition. In the Lion House were 'Prince' and 'Pasha', two beautiful Cape Lions. There was also a good collection of other animals in the menagerie.

By 1961, when the photograph above was taken, the park had changed significantly, with several new rides and sideshows. The photograph was taken from the cable car ride, which whisked passengers from the beach level, to the upper areas of the park. The Beatles also around this time played the Tower Ballroom; this was proof of how popular New Brighton was at the time. The Beatles final appearance at the Tower Ballroom took place on Friday 14 June 1963 on a special NEMS Enterprises presentation of their 'Mersey Beat Showcase' series. The Beatles were supported by Gerry & the Pacemakers and five other groups.

Disaster struck in 1969. The fire, the fourth that the tower had suffered, started on Saturday 5th. April 1969. The call was received at Wallasey Fire Station just after 5am in the morning. The manager and staff had left the building the night before about 8-30pm. after a routine check, the stage area was not included in their check! A police constable discovered the fire in the stage area in the west wing of the tower early next morning.

There had been four fires at the New Brighton Tower grounds since it first opened in 1898. The last came in 1969, being the most destructive which led to its final demise.

The First Fire at the Tower

Builders were still working on the higher portion of the tower structure even though the Tower grounds had just opened in 1898. To protect the crowds below the workmen had placed wooden planks around part of the building to prevent injury from falling bricks etc. On 1 April 1898, shortly after 10 pm, Wallasey Fire Brigade were called out who rushed to the scene to find that the wooden planks 172 feet up were ablaze. Their Manual Pump was not powerful enough to reach that height so the Birkenhead and Liverpool Fire Brigades were asked to attend with their Steam Pump.

Birkenhead Fire Brigade agreed to attend but firstly had to obtain permission to leave their Borough from the Council and Liverpool had to wait for the Luggage Boat to steam up. Whilst both Brigades delayed in attending, the Wallasey Firemen had already climbed onto the planks and were tackling the flames.

Tragically a young Volunteer Fireman, Jim Shore, a bricklayer from Seacombe, fell 80 feet to his death after losing his footing while attempting to reach the fire. By the time the other Brigades had arrived after midnight the fire had burnt itself out.

Measures were taken to improve the Fire Service after the death of the Wallasey Fireman. It was decided that the Manual Pump would have to be replaced by a modern Engine and an order was placed for a new Shand Mason Horse-Drawn Steamer.

The Second New Brighton Tower Fire

The second fire happened on Thursday evening on 20 January, 1955. Fire broke out in the cafe on the third floor and, protected only by a wall, nearly spread to the large ballroom. The fire was reported by the Ballroom Manager, Cyril Isherwood, at 7.25 pm and, with the watchman, John Williams, tackled the fire with a mobile extinguisher until the Fire Brigade arrived. The Wallasey Fire Brigade arrived within minutes and fought the blaze that was over 60 foot from the ground. The flames rose to 25 feet whilst the firemen tackled the blaze from two sides of the building. Three Appliances poured water through the office window and after fifteen minutes the fire was under control. The Catering Manager's office was destroyed.

The Chief Fire Officer, Joseph Holt, said "If the fire had not been discovered when it was, the whole Ballroom would have been involved and the flames might have spread up the building, as well as below, if they had reached a lift shaft nearby. This would have acted as a flue".

The Third New Brighton Tower Fire

The third fire at the New Brighton Tower, which had broken out in the Social Club and spreading to the Ballroom, was reported by the general foreman, Alex McIntyre, at 7.30 pm on 17th August, 1963. After raising the alarm, Mr Intyre lowered the theatre's safety curtain and asked the early dancers to vacate the ballroom. The Amusement Park was also cleared. As many as 26 Appliances and 160 men from Wallasey, Birkenhead, Cheshire, Liverpool and Lancashire Brigades were involved in tackling the fire.

For four hours the firemen tackled the flames and prevented it from spreading to the ballroom but the clubroom and balcony were destroyed. Deputy Fire Chief, Frank Fradley, who directed the operations said, "At one stage it was touch or go whether the entire
287

building would become involved but everyone did a magnificent job".

The Final Fire at the Tower

www.tonyfranks-buckley.com

On Saturday 5 April, 1969, a call was received at 05.08 am that a fire had erupted at the New Brighton Tower. The night before, the manager and staff had left the building at 8.30 pm after a routine check but the stage area, which is believed to where the fire started, was not included.

The fire brigade were soon on the scene and were met with large bellows of smoke pouring out of the windows and sections of the building collapsing. With the collapse of the wall it exposed the Ballroom and theatre to the open air and it allowed the flames to reach other parts of the building. Matters were made worse by the fact that the Tower Boating Lake had been drained so the Fire Brigade had major difficulties in obtaining water. Three relays had to be used to pump water from Marine Lake which was some distance away.

With the lack of water it was soon apparent that the Ballroom would be a complete loss. Parts of the roof began to collapse and there were two blasts on the fifth floor as compressed oxygen and dissolved acetylene cylinders were exposed to the fire. Luckily no one was hurt. Firemen had managed to get into the building from the south to the staircase but could go no further due to falling debris from the collapsed roof. Soon after 7.00 am, less than two hours after the alarm had been raised, there were 25 pumps at the scene of the fire and relief crews were being called in from Birkenhead, Liverpool, Chester County and Lancashire County with over 150 firemen being at the scene with 20 pumps and four Turntable Ladders.

The Chief Fire Officer, Mr E.E. Buschenfield, sent for five more Pumps but it was obvious that fire crew's lives were in danger as the blaze became far too serious to tackle so a decision was taken to allow the building to burn. It was the end of the Tower.

In all, 1191 Firemen and 37 Officers had fought the fire. There were 25 pumps, four Turntable Ladders, a Snorkel, a Heavy Water Unit and a Control Unit at the scene.

An examination of the burnt out remains was not possible due to the condition of the remaining walls. The Deputy Fire Chief, Alec

293

Dean, said: "A thorough investigation of the cause of this fire was made by the fire department in consultation with the Home Office forensic department and the Cheshire County Police. After the elimination of the possible causes it seems that this fire was due to unauthorised entry to the building and subsequent vandalism or accident in the ignition of the stage area caused by vandals. There could have been no other cause. Electricity and gas had been cut off so these were eliminated and there was no other source. There was a lack of direct evidence to pinpoint vandals but it is the only source that was left".

Steps were soon taken to have the charred shell of the once proud New Brighton Tower building demolished.

In the 1970s, the area where New Brighton Tower once stood was redeveloped as River View Park.

Sadly the Tower Ballroom fire in 1969 became the end of an era in New Brighton which never recovered or rebuilt after the incident. The fire was the end moment for the area with the fairground closing immediately, leaving only the New Brighton Palace as a place for small entertainment compared to the delights that had been previously on offer before the fire.

New Brighton Palace

In June 1876 a new company was formed, it was called *The New Brighton Palace Co* and it had a share capital of £100,000. The aims of the company were to build a new entertainment centre in the up and coming resort of New Brighton. Land alongside the beach was acquired and work started on laying the foundations for the buildings; however work soon came to a stop and it seemed unlikely that the project would be completed. A local resident, Mr Laurence Connolly saw the possibilities and bought the site, he completed the buildings and the Palace opened in 1880. In the winter of 1880 a new salt water bathing pool was added. During the 1882 season, the Palace averaged 10,000 visitors per week. Major changes were made for the 1883 season.

The Liverpool Mercury for 22nd March 1883 described it as follows:

The Palace, Winter Gardens and Grotto, which have been built by Councillor Connolly, promise to prove a highly popular place of recreation amongst the many holiday makers who visit New Brighton47 in the summer months. Extensive alterations and improvements have been carried out during the past winter, and every effort has been made to render the Palace and its accessories a thoroughly attractive pleasure resort.

The whole covers an area of about three acres, a portion of this space being occupied by splendid sea water baths. In the Palace proper, the "great hall" which has an area of 22,000 square feet, has been completely re-decorated since last season, and has been converted into a charming salon for music and dancing. The walls have been painted by Mr T.W.Grieve, of London, who has depicted a succession of picturesque views of English and Irish scenery from Kildare to Richmond.

The ceiling has also been elegantly decorated, and the columns and pilasters have been adorned with mirrors. In the Winter Gardens the greenhouses have been plentifully stocked with tropical and other plants, and they already look bright and beautiful with a variety of blossoms. A spacious open air skating rink has also been constructed on the roof of the concert hall, there has also been provided a recreation ground for children, a well stocked aviary and monkey house, and a smaller concert hall.

The most attractive addition, however, is an agreeable grotto, which will afford a cool and refreshing retreat in warm weather. It has been constructed by Mr James Cross of Southport and Manchester, and measures 140 feet by 120 feet. The grotto contains a large waterfall, extending from end to end, a distance of 131 feet, and several cascades intertwined with enarchments. Between the archways play fairy fountains of Swiss design. In the

---

centre is a recess constructed of coral and other grotesque formations, and in the middle of the recess a fairy fountain showers crystallised sprays of water.

Rugged rock work, relieved with rich ferns, gives the grotto a charming aspect, and the effect is enhanced by the water-jets from many fountains of varied designs erected at different elevations. The crypt is supported by over forty iron columns, all richly embellished in rustic fashion to represent trees, and these have been surrounded with hardy ferns and mosses of various kinds, whilst the fountains and artificial rivulets have been abundantly supplied with mosses, lichens and aquatic plants, numbering altogether over 12,000. Two advertisements were placed in The Era, a London based weekly paper covering theatrical matters, in January 1883, the first offering for rent 1,600 square yards at the Palace for a Circus or similar; the second advert was looking for "New and Sensational Entertainments and Side Shows" for1883 the season.

The opening on Good Friday 1883 was marked by a grand concert and a variety show. This was the pattern followed for many years with entertainment of all types being provided, from classical music to variety. As the reputation of the Palace rose, due in no small part to the quality of the sacred music concerts on Sunday afternoons, many famous classical musicians and singers; and many popular variety acts appeared. In order to perform a play in those days, a licence was required. The Palace applied for a licence in 1887, but the request was turned down. In 1896 the building was bought by a Manchester syndicate who planned to build a giant Ferris wheel on the roof. The wheel would have had 42 carriages, each of which would have held 40 passengers. This was never built. When the tower theatre opened in 1898, business at the Palace was drastically affected but the theatre managed to keep going, in 1903 to increase the number of patrons, it became the first hall in Wallasey to show animated pictures.

Liverpool Mercury, Monday, 15th April, 1895

This popular place of amusement was opened for the season on Saturday, and throughout the day it was crowded with pleasure seekers, a fact which augurs well for a successful season. Many improvements have been carried out in the extensive buildings with a view of enhancing the pleasure and comfort of visitors. The commodious ballroom, where a full band plays for dancing, is charmingly decorated throughout, as also is the large and cosy theatre. The grotto, which will have a special attention paid to it during the season, together with the open-air terraces, will certainly prove most attractive to those who wish to take a stroll after leaving the ballroom. There are also well stocked aviaries, a shooting gallery, and several other attractions in the place, which will enable visitors to spend a most enjoyable time. Mr. C. Gray Smith, the secretary and manager who catered so well at the Palace last year, is again at the head of affairs, and on Saturday provided a treat for his patrons in the shape of an excellent concert in the theatre, The artistes were Miss Marie Burnett (soprano), Madame Emile Young (contralto), Mr. George Barton (tenor). Mr. Eaton Batty (baritone), and Mr. William Pagan (humorist). There was a large audience present at both the afternoon and evening concerts, and each item of the programme was much enjoyed, whilst in several instances encores were demanded. The theatre orchestra accompanied the various items in a satisfactory manner, under the leadership of Mr. J. Clayton. For today (Monday) further attractions are provided. Entertainments will be given in the grotto by Deskaro, the juggler, and in the rink by Sizi and Casea, acrobats. In the theatre, both afternoon and evening, will appear the Four Aubreys, sketch artists and horizontal bar performers; Patty Yole, song and dance artist and banjo soloist;

the Ediinsm sketch artists; Rose Harvey, contralto vocalist; and Winifred Yates and and Robert Emslie, who will contribute vocal tableaux vivant's. As regards the future engagements at the Palace, Mr. Smith has made arrangements with some of the best known music hall artists to appear during the season, so that this place of amusement should prove attractive to all visitors to New Brighton.48

In 1907, Wallasey Corporation used its powers under the Tramways and Improvement Act to buy the notorious 'Ham and Egg Parade' and most of the other properties, including the Palace, which fronted onto the river. A new, wider, parade and sea wall were built. The newly formed Tivoli Company took control in

48 Liverpool Mercury, Monday, 15th April, 1895

1913, their plan was to rebuild the Palace and build a new arcade and hotel, and however these plans were abandoned when problems arose over the building of the Tivoli theatre. The next tenant was Mr Ludwig Blattner who renamed the building the Gaiety and carried out many improvements. Towards the end of the nineteenth century, a Birkenhead rope maker named George Wilkie joined a travelling fairground. After 12 years with the fair, he leased at least part of the Palace site and set up a fairground.

A Joy Wheel was located next to the theatre; Joy Wheels were a popular, though short-lived, novelty rides in the early part of the twentieth century. Riders sat on a low, conical disk in the centre of the enclosure, the disk rotated at increasing speed, gradually throwing the riders off. The wheel was surrounded by tiered seating to enable spectators to watch.

In 1916 much of the site was destroyed in a disastrous fire, only the theatre and the skating rink were saved. There is little information on the Palace complex at this time, but it seems likely that the site was split up into a least two parts, the theatre being run by Mr Blattner and rest of the site by Mr Wilkie. There are also very few records as to what was in the fairground, although it is known that Mr Wilkie bought a second hand Burrell Traction Engine after the First World War The cinema, which by now had a separate entrance in Virginia Road, closed at the end of 1926.

In 1936 Mr Wilkie demolished what remained of the old Palace complex and put up a new building to house an indoor fairground. The building was called the New Palace and was completed in 1939. While a new roundabout was being built on the promenade, workmen discovered some unmapped caves, Mr W Wilkie had the caves dug out and constructed blast proof rooms in the caves. A munitions factory was set up and production started in March 1942. The weekly output of the small factory under the promenade was 250,000 machine gun bullets, 25,000 shells and 1,400 press button switches for aircraft radios. After the Second World War, the indoor fairground prospered, and in 1949 the Willkie's opened a circus on a piece of land next to the New Palace (the area which would later be occupied by the Bright Spot amusement arcade).

Some of the rides remained in the New Palace for many years; one of the best known of these was 'The Jets'. The Jets were an early example of a 'rider-controlled' machine, the rider used a lever to control a pressure valve which raised and lowered the arm. The machine in the New Palace was the third one built, and was bought new in 1955. The Jets remained in the New Palace until 1995 when it was sold.

Over the years the ride was 'modernised', the original 'jet planes' were replaced with 'space ships', and the lattice arms were panelled. Another long standing ride was the Waltzer; this was originally built in 1938 and was bought second-hand by Mr

Wilkie, in 1950. This was the last Waltzer built before the Second World War; the Waltzer was sold in 1997. Both these rides are now in preservation, and it is a testament to the care given to these machines that they, and many other rides owned by Wilkie, are still in existence. Other rides didn't stay as long in the fairground, Wilkie bought his 1959 Autodrome second-hand in 1985 and it only remained until 1990.

In the 1960s, as with everywhere else in New Brighton, trade at the New Palace fell off. The fair struggled on for many years but by the 1980s things were getting desperate. In the late 1980s David Wilkie took over running the New Palace and much of the fairground was cleared out to make space for a go-cart track to be built. This brought in new customers and improved the situation.

The go-cart track was closed in 2001, and David Wilkie had the Bright Spot arcade and much of the New Palace demolished. The facade and the shops at the front remained. The New Palace, now an outdoor fairground, continues still under the control of the Wilkie family. The Bright Spot has now been demolished and replaced by a small outside fairground. The building now also houses a night club as well as the traditional cafe with a donut stall catering the indoor arcade housed inside the remaining part of the building.

New Brighton Football Club

New Brighton 1948-49

The once flourishing holiday resort of New Brighton with its excellent beaches, now a housing dormitory for Liverpool, was a town day trippers would flock to just before the turn of the twentieth century. The Tower dominated the skyline, a structure that rivalled the Eiffel version in Paris and its attractiveness was added to with the provision of fairgrounds and amusement parks. Summer events were staged at the Tower Athletic Ground in the shadow of the impressive structure. In order to provide a winter attraction to New Brighton local businessmen clubbed together to launch their own football team early 1897 by the name of New Brighton Tower FC. Not formed for a change by a bunch of cricketers, rugby players or schoolboys, but by a business organisation with little more than pure commercial intents.

There was a certain degree of resentment towards New Brighton Tower, a club apparently intending to buy their way to the top. Therefore the team were accepted into the Cheshire League only, at the time considerably lower-rated than the neighbouring

Lancashire League. Despite this setback, New Brighton Tower managed to attract first-class players to assemble a suitable team that soon became known as the 'Team of Internationals' in newspaper reports.

New Brighton Tower played their first Football League game in Division Two in 1898. The 'Towerites' as they were officially nicknamed, took on Gainsborough Trinity clad in white shirts with blue trimmings and blue shorts. Their League days were to be short-lived. The 'Towerites' were on the brink of promotion in 1899 but that was not good enough for our business friends who had demanded First Division football from the beginning. The 1899/1900 season petered away into indifference in front of meagre attendances. New Brighton Tower's directors vowed to make one last determined effort for promotion in the next campaign.

The 'Towerites' kicked off their 'do or die' season in wonderful salmon pink shirts with black trimmings and white shorts. Rarely attracting more than 3,000 crowds to the Tower Ground the team again missed out on promotion. Alas, as a result English top-flight football has never seen salmon pink shirts. The business venture that was called New Brighton Tower finally folded in August 1901.

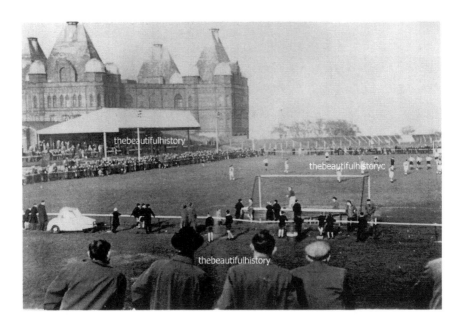

Liverpool Mercury Saturday, 23rd December, 1899

Holiday Fixtures Christmas Day

The League - Division II

Grimsby Town v. Chesterfield, Grimsby
Lincoln City v. Woolwich Arsenal, Lincoln
Leicester Fosse v. Loughborough, Leicester
New Brighton Tower v. Sheffield Wednesday, Tower Grounds,
New Brighton49
Walsall vs Barnsley, Walsall

---

49 Liverpool Mercury Saturday, 23rd December, 1899

Senior football came back to the tip of the peninsula by the turn of the 1920's. Just over on the other side of the Mersey, South Liverpool were struggling, who found themselves with no ground after having left the Dingle Park Ground and a full set of Lancashire Combination fixtures to fulfil. The club transferred across the Mersey to a willing set of football enthusiasts rather than commercial sharks. It was suggested that the club should be called Wallasey Town FC but in fact were renamed New Brighton. They inherited the first colours of their predecessor and played in white shirts with blue trimmings and blue shorts with a shielded 'NBAFC' monogram when they were elected to the Football League in 1923 along with Durham City to fill two vacancies in Division Three North. Heavy rain showed that the Wirral support was fickle with only 3,000 turning up for the first game at Sandheys Park. The location of this enclosure near Rake Lane inspired the nickname 'The Rakers'.

Worthy of note was an FA Cup clash at this ground in 1927 against the illustrious Corinthians who sported gold, white and purple striped shirts due to a colour clash with 'The Rakers'. When New

Brighton reached a low ebb in 1936 they changed to red and white striped shirts with blue shorts in an attempt to change fortunes.

New Brighton's future looked bleak after the hostilities of World War II ended. The club's ground was taken over by the council to build houses to replace those lost in the war. They were also without any playing gear or any equipment and all the club had left was its precious Football League membership and a willing band of volunteers who managed to secure their predecessors' Tower Ground and the purchase of maroon shirts with white shorts. Meanwhile they retained their nickname despite their geographical move. In 1947 they made the history books when a player shortage saw 52-year-old manager Neil McBain turn out in goal to become the oldest player ever to appear in a Football League match.

Yet another change of colour in 1950, this time to red shirts with white sleeves and white shorts, couldn't prevent New Brighton from losing its League status one year later to Workington. Despite more financial problems and regular ground moves, the club survived through to the 1980s but shut down in 1983 when they were playing on unenclosed grounds in the Wirral League. New Brighton FC started up again and played their games at Harrison Park, New Brighton. They have won and been runners up in several local cup competitions, and received an award for best programme in the regional football league. The club is making every possible step to find their own ground, and to be recognised as 'The Rakers' once were. With their history, however, it is perhaps surprising that they aren't called "The Chameleons". However following the 2011/12 season, the committee stepped down with nobody filling the void which has seen the withdrawal of both senior teams from the West Cheshire Divisions.

Guinea Gap Baths

Guinea Gap Baths in Seacombe is the oldest pool on the Wirral. Seacombe promenade was the third stage linking Seacombe and New Brighton by one long continuous promenade. Before the promenade was built (1901), there was a break in the riverbank known to locals as "Guinea Gap". This was a popular place for anyone wishing to go for a swim as it was free from dangerous currents that lurk in the river itself. It was in this place that Seacombe and Egremont Swimming Club was founded back in 1890, they held meetings and competitions there as often as possible. The name of the club was later changed to Wallasey Swimming Club in 1913 and has remained as that since.

The area where Guinea Gap Baths now stands was bought by the council in 1905. Originally there were four houses on this site, these buildings where demolished and the construction of Guinea Gap Baths began in 1906. Guinea Gap Baths where opened by Mr.T.V.Burrows, Chairman of the Health Committee on the 7th April 1908.

For many years this was a favourite local swimming venue and family meeting place, this elegant Edwardian building has graced the Mersey riverbank and still does today instead of what could have been (maybe those nasty "luxury flats" that nobody likes). Almost all local people share memories of learning to swim there, of taking their children to be taught how to swim there, of joining a swimming club there, or of taking part in their first swimming gala there.

There are various rumours as to how Guinea Gap received its name, the most popular theory being an account of the amount of golden guineas from the reign of William III and others found by workmen around 1849 (possibly a pirate's treasure, wouldn't that be an exciting thought!). Another explanation for the name "Guinea Gap" comes from the word "Gyn" meaning "gap in the cliffs"; a small river once ran into the Mersey from this point.

Since 1908, Guinea Gap Baths has enjoyed a colourful history. It has miraculously survived two world wars and during World War I even served as a rehabilitation hospital for the wounded soldiers being cared for at a makeshift hospital in Wallasey Town Hall. That is one of the things we at Wallasey Swimming Club are most proud of.

Guinea Gap originally had sea water in it rather than the chlorinate water pools have today. Its supply of sea water was drawn from the Mersey estuary. This fact may have been the key to the mystery that grew up around the baths. Although there were other saltwater pools, Guinea Gap alone became famous throughout the country for the huge number of national and international swimming records broken there. Excellent coaching and supreme effort from all the swimmers led to these record breaking results. Between 1908 and 1957 no fewer than 205 world and national swimming records were achieved at Guinea Gap Baths. Believe it or not,

Guinea Gap Baths has also been a temporary home for some dolphins. If you don't believe it, just scroll down to the bottom of this page to see the video!

In 1990 Guinea Gap underwent an ambitious refurbishment. The Gala Pool was converted into a freshwater leisure pool for family swimming. A Riverside Conservatory was also added, where you can sit and enjoy the views over the Mersey to Liverpool, while watching your children having fun in the pool, or perhaps just sit and drink a cup of coffee after a nice relaxing swim. The 25yard Training Pool was upgraded and extended to 25 metres, this was to improve facilities for serious swimmers wishing to compete and those of special needs alike. A new Sauna and Fitness Suite was created to replace the old sauna, originally built in an old air raid shelter.

New Brighton Bathing Pool

New Brighton Bathing Pool was opened on 13th June 1934 by Lord Leverhulme at a cost of £103,240 it was the largest aquatic stadium the world. 12,000 people attended the opening. The pool was built on sand, covering an area of approximately 4.5 acres and was constructed of mass concrete, with the floor reinforced with steel mesh. It was covered with a rendering of white Portland cement with a skirting of black tiles. The pool was designed as to gain as much sunshine as possible, therefore south facing and was sheltered from the Northerly winds. The exterior walls were coated with Snowcrete, with special fine sand from Leighton Buzzard. Lights which lit up under water were placed at the deep end for night bathing.

The Pool contained 1,376,000 gallons of pure sea water, which could be filled or emptied in eight hours. The Pool was filled through the ornament cascade and the water was constantly changed and purified, filtered and chemically treated, at a rate of 172,000 gallons per hour. The plant included chemical tanks, aerator, ammoniator, chlorinator, air compressor, and electric motors for the pumps, etc. A regular supply of water was obtained from the adjoining Marine Lake, which acted as a huge storage and settlement tank. The total filter area equalled 861 square feet. The rate of filtration was 200 gallons per square foot per hour.

The Pool was designed to allow for Championship swimming events, on the south being 165 ft (32 laps to one mile) by 60 ft. The central part of the Pool for general swimming was 330 ft by 60 ft (16 laps to the mile). The overall measurements of the Pool: 6,500 square feet, 330 feet by 225 feet wide. On the north side the shallow area was 330 feet by 105 feet. The Pool could hold 4000 bathers and some 20,000 spectators. The depth of the Pool had an average of 5 feet, but at the diving end was 15 feet.

The Baths were also famous for annual events that were held within the complex most notably the "Miss New Brighton" contest. The Miss New Brighton Bathing Girl Contest started in the Pool in 1949 when the first heat attracted only nine entrants. The following heat saw an increase to 23 entrants. The final was won by Miss Edna McFarlane and as the rain teamed down she collected her cup and a cheque for £75, 15,000 people paid to watch the event.

Among the winners of Miss New Brighton, Violet Petty became the holder of the title in 1950 entering whilst on a day trip from Birmingham at the age of 18, she later became known to millions as Anne Heywood the Rank film actress. The last Miss New Brighton contest was held in 1989. Not only did the baths hold local events, there was a major rock event also held on the premises. In May 1984 Granada Television staged a £100,000 Pop Spectacular under the title of "New Brighton Rock" with leading groups taking part. It was attended by large crowds and screened on ITV on Saturday 23rd June 1984 at 10.30 pm.

OPEN AIR BATHING POOL. NEW BRIGHTON   No. 3503

The admission fees were 6d for adults in the week and 1/- on Sundays and Bank Holidays. Children paid 4d and 6d. Non-bathers were charged 2d. At the end of the opening week over 100,000 people had paid to go into the new pool and on the Saturday, a record was set when some 35,000 people went through the turnstiles. During the first four weeks 350,000 people went in, of whom 87,400 were bathers.

Unfortunately like many old traditional building in Wallasey, the Baths took a direct hit from violent storms. The storms in February, 1990 with hurricane force winds of almost 100 mph caused very severe damage to the Pool when seas forced a hole into the foundations of the Northwest corner of the complex causing the upper structure to cave in. With the cost of about £4 million to repair the damage it was decided by the authorities to demolish the building. The Merseyside Development Corporation bulldozers levelled the site in the summer of 1990.

A pictorial view of the building of the Open Air Bathing Pool between 1933 and 1934

Foundation of the Bathing Pool

Wall of the bathing pool, Aug, 1933

Wall at the deep end, with Rowson St. in the distance, Aug, 1933

Looking north-east from the deep end, Nov, 1933

Entrance to the dressing boxes, Nov, 1933

Looking across to the Lighthouse

Cafe block from the deep end. Jan, 1934

View towards diving board, Feb, 1934

View of the spectators tiers, Jan, 1934

View towards diving board, July, 1934

View towards diving board

View of the administrative block

View of the dressing block, April, 1934

Administrative block and shops, May, 1934

Men's dressing rooms, May, 1934

View towards dressing block

Pump House, May, 1934

View of the Cafe

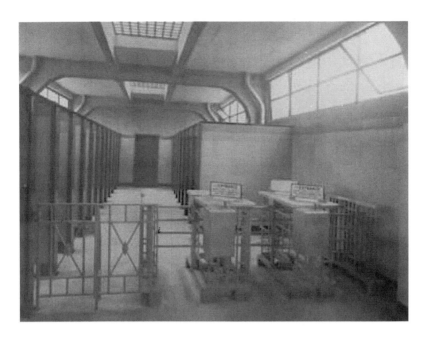

The toilets with one penny turnstile

Changing cubicles

Men's toilets

Fountain

Slide and administrative block

Slide and changing block

The Derby Pool Swimming Baths

The famous Derby Pool stood on Harrison Drive in New Brighton and was named the race course built in the area by Lord Derby around the turn of the 17th Century. Centuries later the race course has long since disappeared but the remains of the Art Deco swimming built in the early 20th century still remains.

OPEN AIR BATHS, WALLASEY. No 3234.

BATHING STATION AND CAFE, HARRISON DRIVE WALLASEY

The huge pool provided many hours of fun for the locals of Wallasey and the day trippers of Liverpool. Its huge outdoor swimming area made the pool an attraction during the summer months and was often the scene of vast overcrowding. Despite its popularity the pool was damaged several times by storm damaged and was eventually shut down due to lack of funds to repair the building in the 1980's.

The building was refurbished many years later and some of the original areas still stand. Today the building is a Harvester restaurant overlooking the bay area and has been given the deserving name of "The Derby Pool".

Disaster

NEW BRIGHTON STORMS –
FEB 1990

Images provided by Richard Littler

The storms in February 1990, seen the end to what was considered the last of the British Seaside Resort in New Brighton. The coastal area was battered with hurricane force winds of almost 100 mph.

The storms caused very severe damage to the New Brighton Outdoor Bathing Pool when seas forced a hole into the foundations of the Northwest corner of the complex causing the upper structure to cave in.

337

With the cost of about £4 million to repair the damage it was decided by the authorities to demolish the building.

The Merseyside Development Corporation bulldozers levelled the site in the summer of 1990.

340

Regeneration

A New Era at New Brighton

Liverpool Daily Post, 19th April 2012

AMBITIOUS proposals to build on the success of the £60m regeneration of a Wirral seaside resort are under consideration.

The Marine Point development has inspired a major boost in the number of people visiting New Brighton. But with the completion of the final phase now largely achieved, Wirral Council officials are now looking at ways to expand the scheme.

The Mersey Frontage proposals aim to develop the area between Fort Perch Rock to Dalmorton Road, as well as the Marine Promenade. They are based around the idea of creating watersports facilities based around a small to medium-sized marina.

Documents seen by the Post also outline the idea of bringing Mersey Ferry services to the resort. They say the whole idea would be supported by an anchor commercial scheme, in the same way the Morrisons supermarket helped developer Neptune create Marine Point.

The Conservative and Liberal Democrat-controlled council has already set aside £1.2m for improvements to New Brighton's roads and pavements. Tony Hurst, chairman of New Brighton traders group Resort, said the plans would be "great if they happen".

But he added: "In the current climate, people are not queuing up to spend money and we have to remember the Neptune scheme took years."

Alan Hayes, of New Brighton residents' association, welcomed the proposals, saying: "It is something which will have to be done. "We have to bring everything up to the standard Neptune has set. They have done a marvelous job."

New Brighton Cllr Pat Hackett said: "It is very important we have a master plan and strategy for New Brighton to build on the success of the Neptune development.50

"I firmly believe we would not be where we are now if we did not have that breadth of vision to make New Brighton a 21st-century resort we can all be proud of."

A council spokeswoman said: "A number of ambitious proposals have been suggested to compliment the regeneration which has already taken place in New Brighton.

"Officers are currently considering the ideas put forward."

---

50 Liverpool Daily Post, 19th April 2012

Thanks to Neptune Developments, New Brighton was given a much needed face lift. The area now has a brand new 1,000-seat six-screen Light Cinema, Grosvenor Casino. A Morrison's Supermarket has also been added along with; Brooklyn's

American style Restaurant, with other facilities such as Starbuck's coffee house, Premier Inn Hotel, with many more building's waiting to be filled. Hopefully this new face lift will draw back tourism to which was once the most vibrant seaside town in Britain.

353

New Brighton In Reflection

New Brighton is a Seaside Resort that is located in the North East corner of the Wirral peninsula. The resort became popular in the 19th century and attracted up to a million visitors each year.

In 1830, a Liverpool merchant, James Atherton, purchased much of the land at Rock Point, which enjoyed views out to sea and across the Mersey and had a good beach. His aim was to develop it as a desirable residential and watering place for the gentry, in a similar way to Brighton, one of the most elegant seaside resorts of that Regency period – hence "New Brighton". Substantial development began soon afterwards, and housing began to spread up the hillside overlooking the estuary – a former gunpowder magazine being closed down in 1851.

During the latter half of the 19th century, New Brighton developed as a very popular seaside resort serving Liverpool and the Lancashire industrial towns, and many of the large houses were converted to inexpensive hotels. A pier was opened in the 1860s, and the promenade from Seacombe to New Brighton was built in the 1890s. This served both as a recreational amenity in its own right, and to link up the developments along the estuary, and was later extended westwards towards Leasowe. The New Brighton Tower, the tallest in the country, was opened in 1900 but closed in 1919, largely due to lack of maintenance during World War I. Dismantling of the tower was complete by 1921.

After World War II, the popularity of New Brighton as a seaside resort declined dramatically. However, the Tower Ballroom continued as a major venue, hosting numerous concerts in the 1950s and 1960s by local Liverpool groups such as The Beatles as well as other international stars. The Tower Ballroom continued in use until it was destroyed by a fire in 1969.

Ferries across the Mersey to New Brighton ceased in 1971, after which the ferry pier and landing stage were dismantled. By 1977, the promenade pier had suffered the same fate.

The nearest airport is the Liverpool John Lennon Airport, and Manchester Airport is not that far away either. If you are a day tripper take the M53 and follow signs to the Wallasey exit, and then follow signs to the New Brighton Promenade.

The height of the glory days have now gone but the resort still remains and offers golden sands and many other leisure attractions and faculties. Even though it once held many theatres it is still home to the Floral Pavilion Theatre and Conference Centre.

Although having to compete with the popularity of foreign package holidays and lack of tourism for many years, New Brighton still boasts the ability to attract day trippers and tourists.

New Brighton has just undergone a £60 million redevelopment scheme -with the Travelodge hotel, Brooklyn's restaurant, Light Cinema and Caffe Cream Ice Cream Parlour and Coffee Shop now open, and also has a casino and more restaurants due to open shortly.

New Brighton has a wide range of attractions and facilities; especially popular are the Riverside Bowling Alley, the Laser Quest centre, and the New Palace Amusement Arcade - which includes a small fairground.

Along the coast, there is Fort Perch Rock, which is a coast battery defence that was opened in the 1830s and became the defender of Liverpool. The Fort is open throughout the year. It features an Aviation and Archaeology Museum, as well as a 'Luftwaffe over Merseyside' permanent exhibition. There is also Perch Rock lighthouse and has Vale Park further along the promenade which includes the Bandstand which for several centuries has played live music.

New Brighton is the quintessential seaside town, and makes a great day out for families, and for people looking to experience traditional fun. I would advise you to get the Ferry from Liverpool to New Brighton but as we no longer have a pier you will need to get off at Seacombe. But that is not all bad news; Wallasey has one of the best coastal walks in Britain. The view across the River Mersey is breath-taking and the view has seen the Liverpool skyline change throughout the years following their own recent regeneration since they were awarded Capital of Culture in 2008.

As well as the spectacular views, the Seacombe to New Brighton Coastal Walk gives people the chance to see where Mother Redcaps was situated and how it became a haunt for Pirates and Smugglers in the 17th and 18th Centuries. Mother Redcaps is now gone but the original stone archway still remains.

If you want a quiet time away from all the bustling tourists, the Gorsehill Millennium Green is New Brighton's spot for local people and visitors to relax and reflect. Near there, there is St. Peter and St. Paul's Catholic Church known as the dome from home as called by sailors on return from sea. It is also a great historical photo opportunity, not only of the church itself, but of the extraordinary view of the Mersey and Liverpool that the spot offers. To get there, walk up Atherton Street to reach the top.

Accommodation wise, there are various hotels in New Brighton, especially the new Travelodge on the Water front at Marine Point. Wellington Road is also an ideal place for cheap Bed and Breakfast but if you want to go a bit more up class then the Grove House Hotel or the Leasowe Castle is ideal. Bus routes also run from the front if you want to explore the surrounding area such as Liverpool and the West Wirral Coastline.

In reflection, New Brighton, though no more in its glory days as a packed seaside resort in the 19th century, is nowadays still a great place for short breaks and day trips, the regeneration has brought back more interest into the area and is still a great place to spend a family holiday in the summer, were days on the beach can be a truly rewarding day for next to nothing. New Brighton still shines Bright. Come and learn our Heritage and great History, it is an area that you will never forget.

Bibliography

1, *Recreation and the Sea* edited by S Fisher (Exeter: University of Exeter Press, 1997)

2, *The Blackpool landlady: A Social History* by JK Walton (Manchester University Press, 1978)

3, *The English Seaside Resort: A Social History 1750-1914* by J K Walton, (Leicester University Press, 1983)

4, *The Englishman's Holiday: A Social History* by JAR Pimlott (Flare Books, 1976, first published 1947)

5, *Brighton: Old Ocean's Bauble* by EW Gilbert (Flare Books, 1975, first published 1954)

6, *Power and Politics at the Seaside* by N Morgan and A Pritchard (University of Exeter Press, 2000)

7, *The English Seaside Resort: A Social History 1750-1914* by J K Walton, (Leicester University Press, 1983)

8, *Leisure in Britain 1780-1939* edited by JK Walton and J Walvin (Manchester University Press, 1983)

9, *2001 Census: New Brighton*, Office for National Statistics, retrieved 19 November 2012

10, Wirral Smugglers, Wreckers & Pirates - Gavin Chappell

11, Philadelphia: A 300 Year History, 1982, Russell Weigley

12, London Morning Post, Wednesday 8th November, 1820

13, Jacksons Oxford Journal, Saturday 11th May, 1822

14, Almost An Island, Noel E. Smith

15 The Inviting Shore, Anthony M. Miller

16 Liverpool Mercury, Monday 27th August, 1860

17 Liverpool Mercury, 20th November 1870

18 Cheshire Observer, Saturday, 10th March, 1860

19 Liverpool Mercury, 7th December 1877

20 Liverpool Mercury, 8th December 1877

21 Liverpool Mercury, 10th December 1877

22 Liverpool Mercury, 13th December 1877

24 Liverpool Mercury, Tuesday 11th June, 1867

25 The Lancaster Gazette, Saturday 20th October, 1821

26 J.S Rebecca

27 Liverpool Mercury, Thursday, May 18th, 1899

28 Liverpool Mercury Tuesday, 27th May, 1890

29 *The Yorkshire Herald Wednesday, 28th May, 1890*

30 Liverpool Mercury Thursday, 29th May, 1890

31 The Dundee Courier & Argus Friday, 30th May, 1890

32 The North-Eastern Daily Gazette Thursday, 30th May, 1890

33 Manchester Times Saturday, 31st May, 1890

34 The Dundee Courier & Argus Monday, 2nd June, 1890

35 The Sheffield & Rotherham Independent Monday, 2nd June, 1890

36 Liverpool Mercury Tuesday, 3rd June, 1890

37 Liverpool Mercury Thursday, 5th June, 1890

38 Liverpool Mercury Tuesday, 10 June, 1890

39 Manchester Times Saturday, 14th June, 1890

40 Liverpool Mercury, Friday 8th September, 1871

41 Liverpool Mercury, Saturday 2nd July, 1892

42 Liverpool Mercury, Thursday 11th April, 1895

43 Liverpool Mercury, Thursday 4th July, 1895

44 Liverpool Mercury, Tuesday 19th September, 1876

45 Liverpool Mercury, Wednesday 29th October, 1862

46 Liverpool Mercury Tuesday, 1st September, 1896

47 Liverpool Mercury, Monday 10th February, 1896

48 Liverpool Mercury, 22nd March 1883

49 Liverpool Mercury, Monday, 15th April, 1895

50 Liverpool Mercury Saturday, 23rd December, 1899

51 Liverpool Daily Post, 19th April 2012

Index

This Page intentionally left blank

12906521R00212

Printed in Poland
by Amazon Fulfillment
Poland Sp. z o.o., Wrocław